Richard's Cork Leg

BRENDAN BEHAN

Richard's Cork Leg

Introduced, edited and with
additional material by
ALAN SIMPSON

Grove Press, Inc., New York

BRENDAN BEHAN
by Alan Simpson

Brendan Behan and I first became acquainted in 1946 after he had been released from political internment in the Curragh Military Camp. We became good friends and in 1954, not long after Carolyn Swift and I had started the Pike Theatre in Dublin, I heard he had written a play which he had sent to both the Abbey and the Gate Theatres. Neither showed signs of presenting it so I asked him to let me read it with a view to production in our tiny theatre.

While I loved the dialogue I found it somewhat repetitive and involuted and in need of some cutting. Brendan was most agreeable about our comments and with a little patient bullying but no acrimony at all we got him to assist in making the necessary alterations.

The Quare Fellow opened in the Pike Theatre in September 1954. The production was greeted mainly with critical acclaim but as the cast was large and the seating accommodation small we could only afford to run for four weeks.

After some time Brendan sent the play to Joan Littlewood's Theatre Workshop. It opened there in May 1956 and was transferred to the West End for a six months' run.

After the initial success of *The Quare Fellow* at the Pike Theatre, Brendan had been commissioned by the Irish language organization, Gael Linn, to write a play in Irish. The result was *An Giall* which proved the most popular work written in Irish ever to be staged at An Damer, Gael Linn's theatre in Dublin. Subsequently Joan Littlewood persuaded Brendan to translate the play into English. *An Giall* became *The Hostage* which Miss Littlewood produced in London, Paris and New York.

After the international success of *The Hostage* and his autobiography (*Borstal Boy*) Brendan's output began to flag. He was drinking heavily and travelling extensively in the wake of various foreign productions of his plays.

Meanwhile Brendan had started on *Richard's Cork Leg*.

5

Sometime in 1964 I was contacted by the New York Theater Guild to know if I would be interested in directing it. However the project fell through as apparently he failed to deliver more than the first act. Not long before returning to Dublin, where he finally succumbed to alcoholism and diabetes, Brendan had spent some time in California and it was there that he wrote most of the rest of *Richard's Cork Leg* in several drafts. However the manuscripts got mixed up with other papers and no one realized that any more existed.

In 1971 I was asked by the Abbey Theatre if I would direct Act One of *Richard's Cork Leg* as a studio production. I agreed, but before going into rehearsal called on Brendan's widow, Beatrice, to see if she could find any other fragments of unproduced dialogue, songs, etc., to round off the projected one-act production. She dug out a pile of manuscripts which I found to be various drafts of a single full-length play incorporating the original Act One of *Richard's Cork Leg* but stopping short just before the dénouement which he had indicated only by a laconic note.

There was little time for a full scale production before the summer break so I did a preliminary editing, and we had a rehearsed reading to an enthusiastic invited audience just before going on our holidays.

       ☆   ☆   ☆

I think I can properly claim that the work I have done on the script has produced the result that would have been arrived at had Brendan lived to see the work staged. Beatrice agrees.

Brendan's enthusiasm for an idea sometimes ran away with him. In one draft Bonnie Prince Charlie produces three tape recordings of voices from the dead. One I gave substance to in the corpse that sings "By the Old Apple Tree" (page 33). Another, a Jewish New Yorker who speaks in a mixture of Yiddish and Irish, I returned to its grave unused. The third voice from the dead, one of Bonnie Prince Charlie's Irish clients, I gave to the spirit of Cronin in the ending I contrived. Brendan's dialogue stopped short at the end of Bawd II's riddle (page 80) : 'a good nun under him'.

Except for a little cutting and a few changes of sequence*
the last scene is much as Brendan left it. He had discovered
from *The Hostage* that a stage party with songs can work very
well if jolly enough and the audience has been well warmed
up. And so it proved in production both in Dublin and London with *Richard's Cork Leg*.

However, although the audience should be aware of a threat
hanging over the hero from both the police and the Blueshirts,
I felt that the exuberance of the party scene might do away
with what little dramatic tension had been achieved by the
shooting episode in the graveyard. For this reason I introduced
the gas, electricity, and dustmen interruptions. I am sure that
the ambiguity as to whether they are police or Fascists would
have pleased the author.

For the benefit of Behanologists and future directors of
Richard's Cork Leg I list hereunder a few of the more enter-
taining divergences or alternative versions which for one
reason or another I didn't use in my own production.

Page 28

BAWD I. . . . maybe he was a spoiled priest?

CRONIN. No, he was a failed drunkard.

BAWD II. I was in a convent one time and our donkey dropped
dead outside the laundry. He must have been thinking
about the other thing because his person was very promi-
nent so to speak. So the gardener said he'd cut it off so as
the children wouldn't be looking at it hanging off the
dead donkey like a man's arm over the side of a boat. So
he cut it off and threw it over a wall, and where did it
land only in the nuns' garden.

BAWD I. Dear me such a place for an ass's baton.

BAWD II. So there it was and the holy nuns came out to walk
round and say their prayers.

* *eg:* The harp sequence (p. 81) came a little earlier. It included the
reference to Beckett, of whom Brendan was very fond.

BAWD I. A beautiful object for them to find in their path.

BAWD II. And this nun sees it and she lets a scream out of her and calls another nun, 'Oh, Sister Dolores, come here and look at this'. So Sister Dolores comes and she calls another nun. 'O Sister Theresa of the Little Flower come here at once and look at this,' and Sister Theresa of the Little Flower lets a scream out of her and calls another nun, 'Oh, Sister Most Holy Passion come here at once and look at this', and they were all standing looking at the donkey's destructor when the Reverend Mother comes out. 'My Children,' she says, 'what is the trouble?' So they point to the ass's tool lying on the path and the Reverend Mother bursts into tears and cries, 'Oh, look what the Protestants did to poor Father Slattery'.

Page 38 – After the quotation from Verlaine on the Belgians:

DEIRDRE. And do you know what Bismark said of the Irish?

CRONIN. No, but like all true Irishmen I like to have my worst fears for my country confirmed.

DEIRDRE. He said that if the Dutch had Ireland it would be a garden and if the Irish had Holland they would all drown.

And a bit farther down:

BAWD I. I know a man was after being on the Continent and he used to love the Swassant Nuff.

BAWD II. What's that?

BAWD I. Heads and heels. It's very complicated.

BAWD II. God knows it is. Another man I knew, he wanted whatever you call it in French.

BAWD I. Swassant Nuff.

BAWD II. He wanted that with complications. I said it was agin the rules of the Gaelic Athletic Association to play foreign games. 'I am not,' said I, 'a Continental contortionist.'

Page 39 – After talking about Crystal Clear, the prostitute who was murdered, Cronin remarks:

CRONIN. Poor Crystal Clear was not avenged by society because she didn't matter.

Page 40 – Beside the speech about the unmarried farmers' pilgrimage to Lourdes, Brendan has scribbled on the margin: 'Lourdes – Haemorrhage of Bad Taste'.

Page 40 – Cronin is discussing how he earns his drinking money selling *Resurrection* (see *page* 7) and selling his Irish National Calendar:

CRONIN (*takes a calendar from his pocket and reads it*). First of January . . . Irish New Year, Easter Monday Anniversary of the Rising 1916 . . . Good Friday King Brian Boru killed at the Battle of Clontarf 1014 . . . here's a more cheerful one, 'Lord Castlereagh cut his throat Aug 12 1822' . . . and I have cards for all occasions, real Irish . . . gloomy and religious . . . this one now (*he takes it from his pocket*) is in the shape of a Celtic cross with snakes and ladders running up and down it, and has written on it 'In memory of the dead, hanged, shot and died in prison for Ireland . . . it's sweet to die for one's country . . . Horace, wishing you a Happy Christmas and a bright and Prosperous New Year.'

Page 53

DEIRDRE. I saw that old man in the coffin. He looked fresh and ruddy and newly shaved. Oh, he was awful. He was like an actor.
CRONIN. O come, come, he didn't look as bad as all that.

Page 77 – After . . . 'the days of the big spitters is over' there was a long rambling passage about various subjects including sexual perversions like necrophilia and sado-masochism, and Ireland. I regret the loss of the following:

CRONIN. You were talking of the men dying for the Republic. They were all healthy men when they died. Mass, breakfast, march out to the firing squad, bang, bang, bang, they were dead. Say if the judge had sentenced them to die of TB or cancer would they have gone so game? To take days and weeks and months about dying.

BAWD I. The minute I hear any mention of Ireland I know the talk will be terribly gloomy.

BAWD II. Ireland and the Republic and dying and suffering always seem to go together.

☆   ☆   ☆

A Note for Directors

Obviously the loose structure of *Richard's Cork Leg* lends itself to a very simple setting, or none at all. However I found that the impact of the outrageous dialogue particularly at the opening was much strengthened by a very realistic setting of a graveyard. Ours was based on actual photographs of Glasnevin Cemetery in Dublin. However, any good representation in three dimensions of the carved extravaganzas of late nineteenth-century memorial architecture that exist would do. The wreaths and plastic 'perpetual flowers' should be as garish as possible to contrast with the sombre greys of the stonework and mouldering marble.

For the first production I engaged the well-known Irish folk group "The Dubliners" who arranged the musical score as well as playing the male roles. Because there were five of them I created the role of The Black Gentleman's Assistant for Barney McKenna. Although this character as played by Barney was beloved of our audiences, he could be dropped in future productions. Before I thought of having "The Dubliners" I had considered using an organ as accompaniment. This could be built into the décor and would enhance the solemn ecclesiastical background. "The Dubliners" play banjo, guitars, melodian, mandolin, violin and tin whistles. However any instrumental combination which suited the talents of the company would suffice.

☆   ☆   ☆

Richard's Cork Leg *in the U.S.*

Immediately after the initial success of *Richard's Cork Leg* I was hesitant about accepting various offers I received to bring the play to America. Because of their heavy international concert commitments, "The Dubliners" would have been difficult to tie down to a long contract. Also I was wary of the euphoria which exists during the Dubin Theatre Festival and often seems to cloud judgements made at that time.

However, when at a much later date I was invited to direct the piece by the University Theater at the Krannert Center for the Performing Arts in Urbana, Illinois (which is 800 miles from New York City), I accepted with pleasure. Here was an opportunity to work further on the play and test its ability to appeal to an American audience without exposure to coast-to-coast publicity and without having a commercial producer peering over my shoulder.

With an all-American cast of students reinforced by a few professionals from the faculty, I got the chance to try out first of all a changed structure of the play *without* "The Dubliners" and secondly to test the ability of the U.S. audience to follow the Irish jokes.

In this I was assisted by Brendan himself. He had written the play after considerable experience of American ways and a residence in New York of several months. Unlike *The Hostage* (which received its first production in the English language in the very Cockney atmosphere of London E15.), *Richard's Cork Leg* is aimed more at the U.S. than anywhere else. Its underlying feeling is intensely Brendan Behan and intensely Dublin, but on the surface the jokes are often trained on American targets.

The play is riddled with ethnic references and the absurdities which seem to dominate contemporary American conversation. The character of Bonnie Prince Charlie could well have come from the satirical pen of Ed Bullins and was much appreciated in Urbana.

Some of the jokes had to be sharpened or words changed to suit American usage. For instance, "Yous'll get us barred" becomes "Yous'll get us bounced." "Corporation Dustmen" becomes "Sanitary Engineers" and so forth.

The main structural change was the addition of six musicians to compensate for the loss of "The Dubliners." The actor playing The Hero (who carries the bulk of the songs) was a professional singer, but we needed a good solid instrumental backing.

To achieve this I multiplied the character of Barney by five and had them speak in unison the lines I had invented for Barney McKenna in London. I also had an organ built into the décor as suggested in my "Note for Directors." The organ did indeed enhance the pseudo-religious songs considerably. The additional "live" Blue Shirts were not strictly necessary, but they very much added to the drama of the Marseillaise sequence (page 65). They were used to mime a montage of Irish revolution from the eighteenth century to present times.

In Illinois where the play opened for a limited run on October 10, 1973, the décor for my production was designed by Don Llewellyn, the lighting by Michael J. Whitfield, and the music was directed from "The Dubliners" arrangements by Bill Keck. The cast was as follows and to them I would like to dedicate this, the American edition. I am sure Brendan would wish me to.

BAWD I (*Maria Concepta*)	Janet Hutchison
BAWD II (*Rose of Lima*)	Camille Hardy
BLIND MEN (*Cronin*)	Steve Retsky
(*The Hero Hogan*)	Mark Bartos
A GENTLEMAN OF A DIFFERENT COLOUR	Larry Venson
THE PADDIES (*Micks, Bogmen, Culchies, or what you will*)	

Don Brearly (Tinwhistle and harmonica),

Jeffery Ganellen (banjo),
Jim Marvin(guitar),
Richard J. Schmalz (percussion)

ORGANIST (*Pianist and Trombonist*)   Bill Keck

THE PADDY'S FAMILIAR   Elisabeth Ann Cabell (violin)

MRS CRONIN   Megan O'Kelly

A CORPSE   Kenneth L. Miller

MRS MALLARKEY   Susan Murray

DEIRDRE MALLARKEY   Cindy Sherman

BLUESHIRT LEADERS, ETC.   Kenneth L. Miller, James Pizer

MOURNERS, BLUESHIRTS, REBELS,
    AND OTHERS   Ken Benda, Michael Baker,
Dale Calandra, George Harrison,
Jim Hinton, Mike Lustig,
Stuart Oken, Mark S. Paulsen,
Michael Wolf

Richard's Cork Leg *was first performed by the Abbey Theatre Company at the Peacock Theatre, Dublin, on March 14, 1972 and subsequently transferred to the Opera House, Cork, and to the Olympia Theatre, Dublin. The cast was as follows:*

BAWD I (*Maria Concepta*)   Eileen Colgan

BAWD II (*Rose of Lima*)   Joan O'Hara

BLIND MEN (*Cronin*)   Luke Kelly

    (*The Hero Hogan*)   Ronnie Drew

A GENTLEMAN OF A DIFFERENT COLOUR
    (*Bonny Prince Charlie*)   Barney McKenna

MRS CRONIN   Terri Donnelly

MRS MALLARKEY   Angela Newman

DEIRDRE MALLARKEY   Dearbhla Molloy

A CORPSE   Ciaran Bourke

BLUESHIRTS, UNDERTAKER'S MEN
    AND OTHERS   John Sheehan
Ciaran Bourke
Ronnie Drew
Luke Kelly
Barney McKenna

Directed by   Alan Simpson
Designed by   Wendy Shea

*The play was also presented by the English Stage Company
at The Royal Court Theatre, London, by arrangement with
Noel Pearson on September 19, 1972 with the following cast:*

BAWD I (*Maria Concepta*)   Eileen Colgan
BAWD II (*Rose of Lima*)   Joan O'Hara
BLIND MEN (*Cronin*)   Luke Kelly
          (*The Hero Hogan*)   Ronnie Drew
A MORTICIAN   Olu Jacobs
HIS ASSISTANT (*Barney*)   Barney McKenna
MRS CRONIN   Fionnuala Kenny
MRS MALLARKEY   Angela Newman
DEIRDRE MALLARKEY   Dearbhla Molloy
A CORPSE   Ciaran Bourke
BLUESHIRTS, UNDERTAKER'S MEN
    AND OTHERS   John Sheehan
                                               Ciaran Bourke
                                               Ronnie Drew
                                               Luke Kelly
                                               Barney McKenna

The direction, design, musical arrangements etc., were the
same as in the Dublin production.

The action, which is in a way continuous, takes place in a
cemetery, in the Dublin mountains and in MRS MALLARKEY'S
house.

The time – well. . . .

There are two acts.

Note: None of the characters in the play (or referred to
therein) bears any relationship to persons either living or dead.
Bracketed sections of the dialogue may be omitted in productions outside Ireland as they are of local interest only.

Act One

This is an Irish cemetery. There are the usual crosses, headstones and tombs and a large statue of Christ. There is an arch with the inscription, 'I Am the Resurrection and the Life' and beside it a board reading 'Forest Lawn Credit Cards Honored Here'.

A singing group dressed as undertaker's men and a priest ken or sing a funeral dirge which should be good enough for the audience to take seriously.

Two veiled figures can be seen, one each side of a big Celtic cross, in bowed attitudes of what appears to be deep mourning. They weep.

Suddenly the group break into 'The Other Night I Got an Invitation to a Funeral'.

> The other night I got an invitation to a funeral,
> But much to my discomfort sure the fellow didn't die,
> Of course he was dissatisfied at having disappointed us,
> And as soon as he apologised we let the thing go by,
> The night of the misfortune, he took us down and treated us.
> He called a quart of porter for a company of ten,
> When some poor chap enquired to know whose money he was
>   squandering,
> The poor chap got his two eyes put in mourning there and
>   then.
> Then Mulrooney struck MacCusker and MacCusker struck
>   some other one,
> And everyone struck anyone, of whom he had a spite,
> And Larry Doyle, the cripple, that was sitting doing nothing,
> Got a kick that broke his jaw for not indulging in the fight.

BAWD II. Here! Give over! Give over!
BAWD I. Stop it, can't you. No respect.

BAWD I. I like a bit of music myself, but there's a time and a place for everything. Not in a cemetery. Yous'll get us barred.

The girls remove black mourning veils and are revealed as Dublin brassers in working gear.

BAWD II. That's one place they won't bar us out of, is the graveyard.

BAWD I. They say this is one of the healthiest graveyards in Dublin. Set on the shore of Dublin Bay. The sea air is very healthy . . . the ozoon, you know.

BAWD II. And there's a lovely view. (*She points.*) Look – the Wicklow Mountains and Bray Head.

BAWD I. Killiney Strand.

BAWD II. I was had be a man, there. The first time. Lost my virginity. He was the prefect in charge of the Working Girls' Protection Society. He said he'd show what I wasn't to let the boys do to me. It was on an outing.

BAWD I. The sea washes up a lot of wreckage on Killiney Strand.

BAWD II. I wonder if they ever found me maidenhead.

BAWD I. Rose of Lima! Have respect for the dead.

BAWD II. They can't hear us.

BAWD I. This is the high class part of the cemetery. Very superior class of corpse comes here.

BAWD II. Well, how did Crystal Clear get buried in it, and she a whore?

BAWD I. Well, that was before the graveyard was covered by the *Forest Lawn credit card.*

BAWD II. What's that.

BAWD I. It's a graveyard in California with a few branches. They investigate foreign graveyards to see their dead don't get mixed up with the wrong class of person.

BAWD II. It's a wonder they didn't go to Glasnevin.

BAWD I. They were going to, but it was too full of revolutionaries.

[They came to Jim Larkin's tomb and they found out he
was in Sing Sing. . . .

BAWD II. Is that in Hollywood?

BAWD I. No, it's a jail where they put Larkin for un-Irish
American activities. Anyway,] these people didn't want their
clients mixed up with him [them] so they came out here.
They do the corpses up beautiful, drawn, dressed and
stuffed.

BAWD II. Stuffed!

BAWD I. They put them in a coffin with a glass front and you can
look at them. They keep them in the chapel here. Oh look,
there must be someone there. Some beautiful, rich American.

BAWD II. Let's go and have a look at him.

BAWD I. I suppose it'd be no harm.

*They walk to the chapel door and go in. Enter at the back of the
stage two blind men,* CRONIN *and* THE HERO. *They wear trench
coats, soft hats and black glasses and have blind men's sticks. They
cross furtively and exit.* BAWD I *and* BAWD II *return from the
chapel.*

BAWD II (*crosses herself*). The Lord have mercy on the dead and
let per-petual light shine upon them, may they rest in pace.

BAWD I (*crosses herself . . . raises her right hand to her forehead*).
Ah, to hell with him (*right hand to her breast*), the old bastard
(*right hand to her left shoulder*), poxy with money (*right hand
to her right shoulder*), he can kiss my royal Iris harse now
(*joins her hands*). Amen, for all the good his money will do
him.

BAWD II. Ah, but he looked beautiful. It's a pity it wasn't a
double coffin – I'd have got in beside him.

BAWD I. Have respect for the diseased departed.

BAWD II. I knew a chap that was out with the Irish soldiers

fighting in the United Nations, and he says the Turks does *that* in graveyards.

BAWD I. Does what?

BAWD II. Does *that*.

BAWD I. God between us and all harm.

BAWD II. Yes, all the whores in Turkey line up at the cemetery gates for the men to bring them in at night time. On the tombstone. They are flat tombstones, of course.

BAWD I (*quickly – to change the subject*). It's a beautiful view from here. Look at the top of the Sugarloaf.

BAWD II. I was coming down off the top of it with a divinity student and there was a crowd waiting at the bottom to give us a big cheer. They were after being watching us through a telescope. I'd fainted with the climb and he was only giving me artificial respiration. The man that was hiring the telescope was charging sixpence a look. 'Interesting views of the hills,' he called it. Then when we came into view, he increased the fee to half-a-crown a look. He offered us a pound to go back up the hill and give an encore.

BAWD I (*impatiently –* BAWD II *has no respect!*). There's some beautiful tombstones here. (*They walk to a tombstone and look at it.*) Ah, here's one here. Put there by a widow. Only one day married.

BAWD II. A one night stand, like Duffy's Circus.

BAWD I (*reads*).

> We were but one night wed,
> One night of blessed content,
> At dawn he died in bed,
> My darling came and went.

BAWD II. '*Came and went*' . . . *dear, dear.*

They turn to look at more tombstones and see CRONIN *and* THE HERO *who have entered, acting very blind, tapping their white sticks.*

BAWD II. Oh, here's the I.R.A.

CRONIN. Good morning, madame.

BAWD I. Good morning, sir.

BAWD II. Good morning, sir.

CRONIN. A lovely morning.

BAWD II. If we had anything to go with it.

CRONIN. What makes you think we are the I.R.A.

BAWD II. Well, on account of being in a graveyard, like. I always think graveyards and patriots goes together.

BAWD I. Don't mind her, sir, she as ignorant as me arse.

BAWD II. How dare you! The cheek of you. I'm a beautiful embroiderer.

THE HERO. Ah, le petit point!

BAWD II. No, mailbags. Above in the 'Joy',* you know.

BAWD I. Rose of Lima! Talking about jail before the gentlemen.

THE HERO. That's all right. I was in jail myself.

BAWD I. Sure, many a good man was. My own father did twelve months for assault ... decent assault, of course. Not the other kind.

CRONIN. I was in myself for rape.

BAWD I. Ah, a political prisoner! Me heart is always with the boys! 'Long live the Republic' is what I always say. Where were you in jail, sir? Me father was in Dartmoor. Mr De Valera was there too, real high class, you know. Look at De Valera now, President of the Republic of Ireland, and he started in Dartmoor with my poor old father. That's what I always say – if you want on, you have to go in. (*Giggle.*) I was in the Joy myself often enough to be President three times over.

THE HERO. No, I was in the Santé prison in Paris. Curious, here the jail is called Mountjoy, and in Paris the jail is called Santé ... [which means sláinte.]

BAWD I. Can you speak French, sir?

THE HERO. A little. I have a great interest in French life, and in the French language, and French letters.

*Mountjoy Prison.

BAWD I (*indignant*). How dare you! How dare you mention such a thing.

BAWD II. In the presence of females. Do you take us for whores?

CRONIN. Certainly. What would you be doing here if you weren't.

BAWD I. The check of you! Who are you, then?

CRONIN. I'll show you who I am. (*He turns upstage and fiddles with the front of his clothes.*)

BAWD I. Oh, Jesus, Mary and Joseph protect us.

BAWD II (*alarmed*). Blessed Oliver Flanagan come to our aid.

BAWD I. He's taking out his weapon! Oh, Mister, we didn't mean to insult you.

BAWD II. The Lord between us and all harm!

CRONIN (*turning to face audience. He has extracted a box from under his trench coat marked 'Help the Blind'*). It's only my collection box.

BAWD II. 'Help the Blind'. He wasn't that blind he couldn't see to rape the poor girl.

BAWD I. Sh! – it's blind he is, not deaf. Anyway, that's a thing that's often done in the dark. That's a nice box you have, sir.

CRONIN. So is yours!

BAWD I (*absently*). Yes, isn't it?

CRONIN (*to* THE HERO). We should be working. Let's get a good pitch and sit down for our begging.

THE HERO. Er, before we settle down, Cronin, I'd like to, er (*He whispers to* CRONIN.) I'd like to, er . . .

CRONIN (*points*). You can er over there. (*He turns* THE HERO *in the direction behind a statue of Christ and* THE HERO *goes off.*)

BAWD I. He walks very sure of himself for a blind man.

CRONIN. Blind balls!

BAWD II. Oh, they'd be interesting. I never seen anything like that.

CRONIN. He's no more blind than I am. (*He takes off his glasses and bows.*)

BAWD I. It's the Leper Cronin!

BAWD II. Maria, you went with a leper.

BAWD I. That's what they called him since the night he leapt over the wall to get out the back of the Bloodpan the night the police raided it. Ah, Leper!

CRONIN. It's yourself, Maria.

BAWD I. We sang together in the choir in the nick in England. I was doing a month for aggressive soliciting, and he was doing two years for – what were you doing that two stretch for, Leper?

CRONIN (*vehemently*). For minding my own bloody business!

BAWD I. Well, there's no need to be so sensitive. Still, it was great sport at mass on Christmas morning, wasn't it?

CRONIN. I remember, Maria. We stood opposite each other at Strangeways where they only had one Chapel for the R.C.'s.

He faces her. BAWD I *faces him.*

CRONIN and BAWD I (*they stand and sing*).

> Angels we have heard on high,
> Sweetly singing o'er our plains,
> And the mountains in reply,
> Echoing their joyous strains,
> Glooo–oo–oo–oo–oo–oo–ria,　⎤
> In Excelsis Deo.　　　　　⎦ (Repeat)

CRONIN *bends his right arm and strikes the crook of his right arm with his left.* BAWD I *bows in acknowledgement.*

BAWD I *makes a deeper bow.*

BAWD II. Oh, beautiful, it was gorgeous.

BAWD I (*to* CRONIN). Who's the beardy looking old fellow with you?

CRONIN. He's called the Hero Hogan and he fought out in Spain.
He was *against* Franco. Now, the Irish crowd that fought *for*
Franco – what used to be known as the Blueshirts are coming
up here to the cemetery to-day to pray for their dead. I'm
here to lead him around and let on that we're just two blind
men. He's going to kick up a row when they start their
speechmaking.

BAWD I. My poor father that was in Dartmoor with Mr De
Valera hit a Blueshirt with a hammer. Split him open. (*Sighs.*)
That was my poor father for you – to God and Ireland true!
Faith and Fatherland. We have the hammer at home, on the
cabinet beside the bottle of Lourdes water, and a picture of
Blessed Evelyn Waugh.

BAWD II. Blessed who?

BAWD I. Blessed Evelyn Waugh. She was a young girl that
wouldn't marry Henry the Eighth because he turned Protestant. (*Absently.*) Amen.

BAWD II. Well, I hope The Hero is not going to hit any of these
Blueshirts with hammers this morning.

CRONIN. You'd never know what he'd do. I don't want him to
know we were talking about him. I wouldn't have told yous
anything only on account of knowing you, Maria. What are
yous doing here, yourselves?

BAWD I. D'you remember poor Crystal Clear that was murdered
out in the mountains. Well, us girls do come out to her
grave on the anniversary of her death. We say a prayer and
sing a hymn for her.

BAWD II. We do always wait till opening time to sing the hymn.
Because that's when we feel she is still with us, bashing in
for a Cork Gin and Tonic, the first of the day. We bring a
little drink with us, and pour a sup on the grave, in solemn
commemoration. (*She nods.*) Here's the Hero. (THE HERO
comes on rubbing his beard.) Here he comes, God bless him
– he has a face like an armpit. I'll lead him over to his seat
to let on you didn't tell us anything, and that we still think

he's blind. (*She takes* THE HERO *by the arm.*) Here you are, sir.

BAWD I (*to* CRONIN). Come on, me little choirboy, I'll lead you in. (CRONIN *and* THE HERO *are led to the flat tombstone.*) Over here. (*They lead the men to the flat tombstone and look down reading the inscription.*) 'Jeremiah Ignatius O'Toole . . .'

BAWD II. O'Toole – a fine manly name, I always say.

BAWD I (*reads*). 'Jeremiah Ignatius O'Toole, and his loving wife, Mary O'Hare.'

BAWD II. 'O'Toole and O'Hare – till death us do part.'

BAWD I. Sit down now with your begging boxes. (CRONIN *and* THE HERO *sit side-by-side facing the audience.*) I always think it's nice to do your work sitting down.

BAWD II. We mostly work lying down.

BAWD I. Rose of Lima! (*To* CRONIN. *He nods. To* THE HERO.) Do you come here often, sir?

BAWD II. Ask me sister, I'm sweatin'!

THE HERO. Not very often. We are refugees from the Paris Metro.

BAWD II. You poor bastard – but that's what you get for mixing with foreign politics.

THE HERO. What do you know about my politics? Who told you?

CRONIN. Nobody told them anything.

BAWD I (*quickly to cover up for* BAWD II's *faux pas*). It's only, sir, we are in a way of meeting a lot of gentlemen and if they don't want a woman you always know they will talk about politics.

THE HERO. Who told you I was that sort of gentleman, as you call it?

BAWD I. Well, I mean, sir, with your beard. If a young unemployed fellow from the flats went 'round like that he'd be arrested.

THE HERO. My entire sympathies are with the unemployed. Everyone should have the right to work.

CRONIN. If they want to.

THE HERO. It's a reactionary lie to say that any of them don't want to!

CRONIN. I'm sorry to say that you're right.

THE HERO. I've never met an unemployed man that would refuse work at trade union wages.

CRONIN. Only one.

THE HERO. Who is that?

CRONIN. You're looking at him (*nudge*) – at least you would be if you weren't blind.

THE HERO. Are you a communist?

CRONIN. I detest the bastards personally, but I like their party, because it's the only one that all the big shots are terrified of. All the big-bellied bastards that I hate, hate the Reds. The only thing that Catholic, Protestant, Green, Trinity College, Ulster Racing Board, Civil Liberties, ex RIC, Conservative, New Statesmen, freemasons, the Orange Order and The Ancient Order of Hibernians, all hate the Reds, so there must be good in their party somewhere. Anyway, why can we not be let walk around and have a drink and a sit down and a feed and a bit of the other ...

BAWD II. Hear, hear.

CRONIN. And a chat.

THE HERO. But say if everyone did that?

CRONIN. Say, if my aunt had bollocks she'd be me uncle.

THE HERO. But could you get no satisfaction from having a job?

CRONIN. A job is death without the dignity. I'm married and with kids. Even though I'm unemployed my wife loves me.

BAWD II. Ah, well, working or idle you can always put a bit in her stomach.

BAWD I. I think weddings is sadder than funerals, because they remind you of your own wedding. You can't be reminded of your own funeral because it hasn't happened. (*Song intro.*) But weddings always makes me cry.

BAWD II (*rises and sings*).

I often think of happy nights,
And of my wedding day,
We'd climb the stairs and say our prayers,
Before we'd hit the hay.
The mattress spring we made it ring,
The night that we were wed,
Ah, grah mo chree, just you and me,
In one big double bed.

BAWD I (*sniffs a tear*). Beautiful, Rose of Lima, your blood's
worth bottling.
BAWD II (*sings*).

The poet talks of country walks,
Beneath the evening star,
And fun afloat on a sailing boat,
Or the backseat of a car.
But I will tell of a quiet hotel,
Where nothing much was said,
But the mattress shook and I took pot luck,
In that big double bed.

A youth came from the country,
Along with his young bride,
'We want a room for our honeymoon'
The landlord, he replied,
'I'll give you the bridal suite'
The youth said 'Have no fears,'
'No bridal at all,
But agin the wall,
I'll grip her by the ears.'

BAWD I. Very affecting.
BAWD II (*sit*). I was here at our baby's funeral, and he came to it
too. We'd been separated a long time, but I thought we would
have been reunited (*cries a little*), over the grave of our little

child. His name was Richard and he had a cork leg given to him be the British Government – a real good one it was.

BAWD I. Oh, fair play to the British – their glass eyes and cork legs is the best in the world.

BAWD II. It was that well made that I didn't know he had an artificial leg. He wore it into bed and all, and I didn't know what it was. Howandever, says I to him, when I felt it beside me, 'Give me a glass of water and I'll chance it'.

BAWD I. Rose of Lima! Before the gentlemen.

BAWD II. They can't hear us.

CRONIN. We're supposed to be blind, not deaf.

A black gentleman crosses upstage.

BAWD II. Oh, there's the beautiful man in the silk dress.

BAWD I. You mean the man in the beautiful silk dress.

BAWD II. Yes, the one that was above in the chapel with the dead stuffed Yank in the coffin.

CRONIN. How do you know the dead man was an American?

BAWD I. There was no smell – only soap.

BAWD I. Yes, that's it. I was had be Yanks. No smell.

BAWD II. That's right. The first one I was with, he put stuff under his arms before he got into bed, I was going to ask him was it me brother he wanted. Here's the man friend now. Oh, he's a black Yank.

BAWD I. No, he's not. He's an Indian, that's what he is. An Indian potentialtate. God, I swear to Christ it's the Bag and Can.

BAWD II. The Aga Khan! Maybe he's looking for recruits for his harem.

BAWD I. We could be white slaves on silk cushions, eating Hadji Bey's Turkish Delight* and drinking gins and tonics. It'd be grand and warm for the winter.

*Hadji Bey founded a Turkish Delight factory in Cork. In England we said 'Fry's'.

THE HERO. He is the richest man in the world, and a great lover of bareback riding.

BAWD II. We were made for each other. Only one thing – is he a Catholic?

CRONIN. He loves horses and he's putting up a memorial to his dead jockey for all the winners he mounted.

BAWD II. It would answer him better to remember all the women he mounted himself.

BAWD I. Behave yourself, Rose of Lima, here comes the lovely gentleman. (*She practises a bow.*) 'Lovely morning, your highness, your majesty, your highness.' Isn't he gorgeous. He must be a class of a pope. Here he is. (*She has a final practice.*) 'Lovely morning, your majesty, your highness, your holiness.' (BONNIE PRINCE CHARLIE *comes down from the chapel door and as he walks to* BAWD II *and* BAWD I *they bow to him. Sure enough he is wearing a beautiful silk garment like a dressing gown, but of a more sumptuous condition than is usual.*) Lovely morning, your majesty, your highness. (BONNIE PRINCE CHARLIE *takes no notice but he walks past her.*) Your holiness.

BAWD II. Your Emminence, Your Worship. (BONNIE PRINCE CHARLIE *signals contemptuously for them to leave his way.*)

BAWD I (*straightens up from her bow and looks after him*). Go along, you black bastard!

CRONIN (*urgently to* THE HERO). Stand up and beg. If we're supposed to be beggars we have to beg. (THE HERO *hastily goes with him and they stand in the path of* BONNIE PRINCE CHARLIE.) Beg. (*To* THE HERO.) Beg, can't you?

THE HERO. Er – succour les aveugles, altesse. Help the blind. Succour les aveugles, altesse.

PRINCE. Certainly, if you are genuine aveugles. Take off the glasses and let me see. (CRONIN *and* THE HERO *take off their black glasses and stand with their eyes tightly clenched.*) Oh, indeed yes. There is a pound note. Get yourself and your friend a drink. (*They stretch out their palms,* BONNIE PRINCE

CHARLIE *gives them nothing but looks down at their palms and walks off.*)

CRONIN (*turns to* THE HERO). Give me the pound note, I'll look after it. (THE HERO *opens his eyes and shows his palms, indicating that he got nothing.*) Where's the bloody pound?

BAWD I. He gave you nothing. He gave neither of you anything. It was his idea of a joke, the heathen whoremaster.

BONNIE PRINCE CHARLIE *waving his hand, laughing a silvery laugh, walks up to the chapel and as he enters he turns his back and we read in bright orange-gold letters across the back of his gorgeous garment the words 'Harlem Globe Trotters'.*

BAWD I. That (*She points towards the spot* BONNIE PRINCE CHARLIE *has just left.*) that racin' crowd is as mean as the grave. They have the first shilling they ever earned.

BAWD I. They have their Confirmation money. There's a lot of them buried here. (*She indicates.*) 'I.H.S.' – Irish Hospitals Sweeps.

THE HERO. Ridiculous. It's a Latin phrase – 'In hoc signum vincit' –

BAWD I. How well you know the Latin. Maybe you are a spoilt priest?

THE HERO. A spoilt bourgeois social democrat.

BAWD I (*knowledgeably*). Ah, a French Order like the Dominicans. Here's a girl coming up the cemetery.

MRS CRONIN *crosses upstage with a tray.*

CRONIN. Is she a nice looking girl?

BAWD II. If you were really blind, wouldn't it be all equal to you what a girl was like?

BAWD I. Bedad it's not, then. A blind man can be very particular. He has the sense of smell.

BAWD II (*goes over to* THE HERO). Smell me. (*She leans over under him and he smells her.*)

THE HERO (*nervously*). Er . . . most agreeable, thank you.

BAWD I. Rose of Lima – you're very common, going round being smelt.

CRONIN. Give us a smell. (*She goes to him and he smells her.*)

BAWD II. Well?

CRONIN. You've been drinking Tullamore Dew.

THE HERO (*bows*). Very good whiskey.

BAWD II (*goes back to* THE HERO *and nuzzles her face into his*). There you are. Your friend doesn't mind the smell of me.

CRONIN. He said he likes Tullamore Dew. I am a judge of whiskey myself.

BAWD II. Is that so? Well, I'll give you a test. (*She takes a small bottle from her pocket.*) Try that.

CRONIN (*takes a slug of whiskey*). It might be Jameson's. No. No, I'd say that was [Paddy's] Johnny Walkers.

BAWD II (*hands him another small bottle*). Here's another specimen, whose is that?

CRONIN (*takes a drink and spits it, in horror*). Oh, oh, you dirty . . . bitch . . .

Enter MRS CRONIN (*pregnant*), *with a tray on which is a pot of tea, a milk jug, sugar bowl, two cups and two large sandwiches.*

BAWD I. Here's that girl. She's coming up here, so she is, carrying a tray of food.

MRS CRONIN. Ah, there you are, dear.

CRONIN. Turn a little to your starboard there. (*She turns left.*) No, no, that's port . . . starboard, I said. (*She turns right and* CRONIN *feels her breasts, etc.*)

THE HERO (*in French*). . . . 'Trebord et basbord.'

CRONIN. Well, they're both there. Did you bring the breakfast?

BAWD I. That's a nice thing. Putting your hand all over a girl and then asking if she's brought your breakfast?

CRONIN. As the lady in question happens to be my wife, wedded according to the rites of the Apostolic Episcopal Church of Ireland . . .

BAWD I. What's that?

CRONIN. That's the Protestant Church. They believe in divorce. It was started by Henry the Eighth.

BAWD I. I didn't know you were a Protestant, Leper, I mean I didn't think you'd be let in.

CRONIN. I'm not really a Protestant, but there's a fund for giving money to distressed Protestants below in the County Kerry, and none of the natives would say they were Protestants. So we got converted and went down to live there and qualified for the money. I wish I could get back to being a Catholic. It's a dangerous way of getting a few quid. Say if I got run over by a motor car, or something? and died in heresy?

MRS CRONIN. Is he the man you're working for? (*She points to* THE HERO *who nods.*) I've brought some for him too.

CRONIN (*to* THE HERO). Eat up. (*Eats himself. Points to* MRS CRONIN.) See that girl there. Mother of three babies. One at her breast. Hasn't broken her fast yet, have you?

MRS CRONIN. No.

CRONIN. Two small babies and another one at the breast, never gets more than a sip of weak tea and a bit of dry bread in the morning.

THE HERO. Can't we give her one of the rasher sandwiches?

CRONIN. Can't be done. (*Rises, to* THE HERO.) Did you say you wanted to reconnoitre a bit?

THE HERO (*as he and* CRONIN *exit, eating*). I suppose we'd better. The Blueshirts will be around at twelve noon.

BAWD I (*to* MRS CRONIN). That husband of yours has a terrible cheek, so he has. Putting his hand up your clothes and practically boasting about starving you.

MRS CRONIN. Do I look starved?

BAWD I. Well, now I come to look at you, you do not look starved.

MRS CRONIN. My husband likes to talk that way before other men. They're so hag-ridden be their wives that he stands before them as a shining example of a dirty heartless savage. And then it sometimes pays the odds. (THE HERO *rushes back on.*) Oh! . . .

THE HERO (*to* MRS CRONIN). Here is – (*He pants.*) Here is . . . (*He puts his hand into his pocket and gives her some money.*) I admire your husband's strength of character. But he is a bit too ruthless for me. (*He hurries off.*)

BAWD I. What did he give you?

MRS CRONIN (*opens her palm*). Two pounds.

BAWD I. Aren't you lucky?

MRS CRONIN. I told you my husband's old carry-on sometimes pays the odds.

BAWD I. Well that was a handy couple of quid.

BAWD II. And she never even opened her legs!

BAWD I. She never opened her mouth.

BAWD II. And we after bringing the Dunlopillo, on the off chance of picking up a bit of loose trade. If you laid it on the flat tombstone, it'd be as good as a bed in the Shelbourne. In the afternoon the funerals will be over and you'd never know what you'd pick up. We'll hire it to you for a pound.

BAWD I. No, no, Rose, this is the Leper's wife.

MRS CRONIN. Don't you call my husband that. Don't, or be God I'll kill you. (*She goes for* BAWD I *who recoils.*)

BAWD I. We didn't mean any harm. Sure, we all like the (*She recovers in time.*) your husband, I mean.

MRS CRONIN (*to audience*). Everyone does . . . except the good living, honest hard-working people. Sure they wouldn't even let him march with the unemployed.

BAWD I. Well, that's a bloody disgrace, so it is! Your husband with his length of service with the unemployed, there is no man in this city more entitled to march. I mean, he is a veteran of the unemployed. Years and years . . . when most of the new crowd was still working.

MRS CRONIN. That's what the Workers' League said. They said he wasn't genuinely seeking employment.

BAWD I. The cheek of them.

MRS CRONIN. But he wasn't genuinely seeking employment. My husband can't work. It's not that he's lazy. He'll get up at five on a summer's morning to go for a swim or a drink down in the markets. But if he gets a job he's in such terror, he can't leave the bed. Once he was offered a job working for a newspaper, and I was delighted, because a man gets a good screw working in a newspaper office.

BAWD I. Indubitably . . . especially if he's on the night shift.

BONNIE PRINCE CHARLIE *enters* [*with his helper* BARNEY].

BAWD I. Here comes the black prince.

MRS CRONIN. Oh, he's a prince, is he?

BAWD I. How the hell would he get the fare over here if he wasn't a prince? I suppose he's a doctor in the Rotunda. (BONNIE PRINCE CHARLIE *comes over*.) Back again, your highness?

PRINCE (*with an Oxford or a Trinity or a Yale accent*). Well actually, I am only a prince in name. My name is Bonnie Prince Charlie, but that's because my surname is Charlie, and my mother thought that Bonnie Prince would go well with it.

[BARNEY. That's right, boss.]

PRINCE. She saw it in a book somewhere . . . I am an ordinary American.

BAWD I. Begod I never heard of an ordinary American before. That must be because you're black.

PRINCE. Certainly not. I'm a fully integrated American. I work here for that great American Institution, Forest Lawn. I would like to tell you about it and I quote . . . I believe in a happy Eternal Life . . . I therefore prayerfully resolve that I shall endeavour to build Forest Lawn . . . as unlike other cemeteries . . . as Eternal Life is unlike death . . . a park filled with sweeping lawns, beautiful statuary, noble architecture . . .

[BARNEY. That's right, boss.]

PRINCE. With interiors full of light and colour, and redolent of the world's best history and romances.

[BARNEY. That's right, boss.]

PRINCE. This is our 'Oirish' branch begob!

BAWD I. Sure it'll give employment anyway.

PRINCE. For those who request it we have tape-recordings especially made of the Loved One's voice, electronically co-ordinated with instruments in the body of the Loved One to give the appearance of life.

[BARNEY. That's right, boss.]

PRINCE. It has proved a great comfort to many Waiting Ones to once again hear the voices of those who have gone before.

BAWD II. Before what?

BAWD I. Arrah, the people who have died before us, of course.

BAWD II (*crosses herself*). Well, thanks be to God they got the start of us.

PRINCE. With your permission I should like to give you an example of this service. (*A helper wheels in a coffin.*)

THE CORPSE (*sitting up sharply, in a mechanical way*). Hi, you all there. I'm just settling down here and I hope my Heavenly Father won't begrudge me a drop of good corn likker. I think I'll sing a song, put a bit of life into the party. You'd think there was someone dead around here . . . heh, heh, heh, that's good that is.

He sings – if you could call it singing.

> By the old apple tree in the orchard,
> It was there that they hung my pappy,

And he's sorry that he growed it,
Gosh, sir, he rued it,
For he died by that old apple tree . . .
Yippp . . . eee

Be seein' you, folks.
Not too soon, *you* hope . . . heh, heh.

THE CORPSE *suddenly lies back in his coffin and is wheeled off.*

PRINCE. And, of course, we are now encouraging the holy Irish
to join us.
[BARNEY. That's right, boss.]
BAWD I. The holy Irish! Ah, listen now, we're not *all* like Matt
Talbot.
PRINCE. Who dat (*recovers*) I mean, who was he?
MRS CRONIN. Ah, he was a very holy man, sir. He died from
the hunger. The Timber Merchants asked the Pope to
make him a Saint, because he refused to take money for
overtime.
BAWD I. The priests say he's up in Heaven and they're after
turning half of Dublin against going up there.
BAWD II. Jesus, I wouldn't spend a night with him, never mind an
eternity.

THE HERO *runs in followed by* CRONIN. *They watch two females
crossing upstage.*

THE HERO. Here's somebody coming. (*Takes off his black glasses.*)
Yes, it is she. My first cousin and her daughter.
BAWD II. You said that in a half-arsed fashion. You should say
'Yes, it's her. My first cousin and my second cousin.'
THE HERO. But it is my first cousin and her daughter, her daugh-
ter, who is not my second cousin, but my first cousin once
removed.

BAWD II. Who removed her?

CRONIN. Do they know you're going to attack the Blueshirts?

THE HERO. No, no. I think she is throwing the ashes of her brother to the wind. He died out in the Congo.

MRS CRONIN. I am sorry for your trouble.

THE HERO. I detested the man. A disgusting Fascist. I am fond of my cousin and her daughter.

BAWD II. Your niece.

THE HERO. My cousin's daughter, damn it! Why have these family distinctions such importance for you? They were only Norman regulations for the distribution of land and wealth, and I don't think your family was troubled much with either of them.

BAWD II. How dare you, you Orange bastard, my people were playing harps and spreading the Gospel and civilization when yours were climbing trees and trying to get a look at us.

PRINCE (*excitedly*). The Irish are proud of their nationality.

[BARNEY. That's right, boss.]

THE HERO. Other people have a nationality. The Irish and the Jews have a psychosis. (*Puts his glasses on again.*)

PRINCE (*to* THE HERO). By the way, sir, does your cousin have permission from the proprietors of this property . . .

THE HERO. The air is free, I presume!

PRINCE. The air may be free but the ground under it certainly is not.

BAWD II. Oh, here is the lady with her box.

Enter MRS MALLARKEY *and her daughter*, DEIRDRE. MRS MALLARKEY *is carrying a wooden casket, probably oak.*

BAWD II. Good morning, ma'am, and you too, miss.

MRS MALLARKEY. Good morning. (*To* DEIRDRE.) Two blind men and two fallen women.

BAWD II. We haven't been doing much falling today.

BAWD I. Shut up, Rose. (*To* MRS MALLARKEY.) Who are you calling fallen women to?

BAWD II. That's right, Maria. Cheek . . . calling falling woming.

MRS MALLARKEY. I am very religious, exceedingly charitable and I have a heart of gold. It's often been remarked upon.

CRONIN (*with further unction*). God and His Holy Mother bless you, I knew that by your beautiful soft voice.

MRS MALLARKEY. But I didn't bring my purse with me, this morning.

CRONIN (*in his low Dublin accent*). Ah, you poxy oul' whoor.

DEIRDRE. What did you say?

CRONIN. I said the lady has a good heart for God's poor.

MRS MALLARKEY. Yes, indeed, I'm famous for it.

BAWD I. Maybe the kind lady has something to eat in the box.

MRS MALLARKEY. I am Mrs Mallarkey and this is my daughter, Deirdre.

MRS CRONIN. Have you got sandwiches in the box, Mrs Mallarkey?

MRS MALLARKEY. No, no, my brother is in it.

BAWD II. How could your brother fit in a little box like that?

CRONIN (*piteously. To audience*). Oh, lead us away from here, from that old woman who keeps her brother in her box.

DEIRDRE. It's quite all right . . . my uncle is in the box. At least his ashes are.

BAWD I. Why didn't he empty his ashes into the bin, like everyone else.

BAWD II. That's right, and not be doing the Corporation dustmen out of a job?

DEIRDRE. They are the ashes of himself. He died and was cremated.

BAWD I. Well, he cannot be buried in a Christian cemetery if he was cremated.

PRINCE (*to* MRS MALLARKEY). In that case, perhaps Mrs Mallarkey, I could be of assistance to you. I represent a memorial park in the United States.

MRS MALLARKEY. Oh, my brother hated America.

PRINCE. Oh, he mustn't do that, baby.

[BARNEY. That's right, boss.]

MRS MALLARKEY. He died in the Congo. (*Takes a photograph from her pocket.*) Here is his picture. (*Hands it to* BAWD I *and* BAWD II.)

BAWD II. The lord of Mercy on him and let perpetual light shine upon him. Why is he wearing them funny clothes?

MRS MALLARKEY. He was dressed as a Belgian Count.

BAWD II. A what?

MRS MALLARKEY. He was dressed as a Belgian Count.

BAWD II. A what?

MRS MALLARKEY. A Belgian Count. 'C-o-u-n-t.'

BAWD II. That must be the new way of spelling it.

MRS MALLARKEY. Yes, he was a Belgian Count, and was murdered by the natives in the Congo.

BAWD II. What did they murder him for?

MRS MALLARKEY. Because he was trying to civilize them. He'd only set fire to two villages when his supersonic jet had to make a forced landing. The natives killed him and the others with spears.

CRONIN. What? No ground to air missiles? Primitive heathens! They had no weapons of civilized war. Poor man he was a gentleman.

MRS MALLARKEY. Our family is descended from a wild goose.

BAWD II. From a wild goose? I'd be nervous of that.

MRS MALLARKEY. You know. The Irish aristocrats who went into exile and took service with the French armies after the defeat at the Boyne.

BAWD I. Ah yes, like Hennessy's Brandy. And you are Belgian, ma'am?

MRS MALLARKEY. Yes, I'm an Irish Walloon.

BAWD I. An Irish balloon, isn't that beautiful?

BAWD II. You are like a balloon in a way.

CRONIN. You know what Verlaine said of the Belgians: 'When

a Belgian is drunk, he thinks he is behaving like a beast, but he does himself an injustice – he is only behaving like a Belgian.'

MRS MALLARKEY. What was that Verlaine said . . . I'm a little deaf.

CRONIN. He said the Belgian showed great bravery in going to civilize the Congo, Roger Casement wrote a report on it.

MRS MALLARKEY. Casement? (*To* CRONIN.) You know that he was a homosexual was proved by the British Government . . . The Committee were all old Etonians who knew about it. And now, my dear friends, I will cast my brother's ashes to the winds.

BAWD II. With the acclamation of one and all.

PRINCE. I think it's not ethical when you haven't made even a small deposit. (*He shakes his woolly head.*)

MRS MALLARKEY (*to* THE HERO). Perhaps, dear sir, *you* would read the eulogy?

BAWD II. He's blind.

BAWD I. Order, please.

THE HERO (*sings*).

> From Brussels' town they came to raise the Congo from the mire,
> And braved with true Crusader's zeal, the rebels' murderous fire,
> To bring the presence Belgique to the savage native clans,
> They fought and bled and never fled, those Belgian Black and Tans.
> A lot of lies by radicals about King Leopold,
> And slanders on the missions and mineowners too were told
> To chastise sullen tribesmen, we amputate their hands,
> We shed their blood for their own good,
> Us Belgian kind Black and Tans.

MRS MALLARKEY *sobs a little.*

DEIRDRE (*puts her arm around her*). There, there, mother.

MRS MALLARKEY. I will open my box.

BAWD II. Three cheers . . . the lady is going to open her box.

MRS MALLARKEY. I will now cast my brother's ashes to the four winds of Erin. (*She opens the box and throws out the ashes. They go into* THE HERO's *face.*)

THE HERO. Oh, snuffle, uffle.

CRONIN (*turns to him and holds him by the face*). Here, what's the matter with you.

THE HERO (*aside*). I never liked him alive and I didn't expect to have to eat the low bastard.

MRS MALLARKEY. What's wrong with the poor man?

BAWD II. Something he ate.

BAWD I. Your brother.

CRONIN (*hits* THE HERO *on the back*). He'll be all right. The next time you're scattering a brother, throw him with the wind.

A bell rings.

BAWD I. Rose of Lima, it's time for a prayer for poor Crystal. (*She and* BAWD II *kneel and bless themselves in an attitude of devotion.*)

MRS MALLARKEY. The girls are praying for their *dead*? They mourn their mother?

CRONIN. No, a prostitute. A colleague, called Crystal Clear. She was murdered up the Dublin Mountains, and there was a police superintendent and a doctor arrested for it. Serves her right for mixing with the police.

BAWD I *and* BAWD II *bless themselves and stand. Both rise.*

BAWD I. All the girls do come, but there's not many here now. There is a lot emigrated to England and America, and then out of what's left, there's a crowd gone over to the Unmarried Farmers' Pilgrimage to Lourdes. There's nobody loves like a pilgrim and we didn't want the Unmarried Farmers wasting their meaning on them atheist bitches in Paris. Rose, get the wreaths. They are under the foam rubber mattress. (BAWD II *goes off and brings back three wreaths.*) We will walk over to the tomb. (*They walk right to the statue of Christ.*)

BAWD II. She's buried with her father. This is the grave. (*Looks up at the statue.*) It's not a bit like him.

BAWD I. That's Our Lord!

BAWD II. Oh, *Him.* It's a very good likeness of *Him.*

BAWD I. Give me the wreaths. (BAWD II *hands her the wreaths and she reads the inscriptions.*) This is from the queers. Real sympathetic they always are: 'Fondest memories of our dear sister. Competition is the life of trade. Love from all at hindquarters' . . . I mean, 'headquarters'.

BAWD II. Ah, beautiful.

BAWD I. And this is one from Belfast. Orange lilies. 'From the Protestant Prostitutes of Donegal Pass.'

BAWD II (*to the others*). They differ from us like, about Infallibility and Transubstantiation.

BAWD I. And of course, they haven't got the Apostolic Succession. But they are good girls. They've a poem with it.

What matter if at different shrines
   we worship the same God,
What matter if at different times our
   fathers won the sod?

BAWD II. Which sod was that? I knew a good many. One was a nice old sod. All he wanted was a little . . .

BAWD I. It doesn't mean that kind of a sod. It means Ireland.

MRS MALLARKEY. They are certainly beautiful wreaths.

BAWD I. And now we are having the little song for poor Crystal.

MRS MALLARKEY. I should like to join in with you. Deirdre
has not got the voice. She takes after her father, who is now
silent forever, thanks be to God.

BAWDS I and II (*piously*). Amen, Amen.

MRS MALLARKEY. Deirdre, you stay and mind these poor afflicted
blind men . . . I will take these fallen women home, and give
them some soup.

CRONIN. Deirdre, look after me.

DEIRDRE. Oh, shut up.

BAWD II. Order for Crystal Clear's song.

BAWD I. The late Crystal Clear.

BAWD II. We called her the late Crystal even when she was
alive, because she worked on the late shift in O'Connell
Street. . . . I never liked it, nothing but drunken journalists
and milkmen.

BAWD I. Rose of Lima. (*She lifts her song sheet.*) Right, now. (*Song
intro.*) Ane, dough, tree*: (*Holding their song sheets* BAWD I
and BAWD II *and* MRS MALLARKEY *sing.*)

BAWD I (*tune – Faith of our Fathers*).

> Here we lay poor Crystal Clear,
> To mind and memory ever dear,
> To mother earth, her clay we mix,
> Beloved of Harries, Toms and Dicks

ALL.

> She is gone but not forgotten,
> Her heart was good, but her luck was rotten,
> By all beloved and held in honour,
> Take out your beads and pray upon her.

* Phonetic version of the Irish for one, two, three.

BAWD II.

> She soothed sinners, softened saints,
> And kissed the congregation,
> To love inclined, with all mankind,
> Of every race and nation.

All except CRONIN, DEIRDRE *and* THE HERO (*who has been seated facing upstage since the ashes choked him*) *turn and process off in a reverend manner as they go.*

ALL.

> She is gone but not forgotten,
> Her heart was good, but her luck was rotten,
> By all beloved and held in honour,
> Take out your beads, and pray upon her.
>
> She soothed sinners, softened saints,
> And kissed the congregation,
> To love inclined with all mankind,
> Of every race and nation.

CRONIN (*on tomb*). They are gone?

DEIRDRE (*turns*). Yes, mother has taken them away for some soup.

CRONIN (*patting tomb*). Sit down beside me and keep a poor blind man company.

DEIRDRE. Well, I have to wait for mother to come back, so I suppose I might as well. (*She sits beside him on the flat tombstone, and he pushes* THE HERO *to make room for her.*)

CRONIN (*to* THE HERO). Here, move up in the bed. I have to push him. He doesn't hear me.

CRONIN (*hugs* DEIRDRE *closer to him*). Well, I suppose I might as well have a go. (*In dramatic tones.*) You have lovely eyes.

DEIRDRE. How do you know? You can't see them.

CRONIN. Well, I have to start somewhere. You know, it's a strange thing, but seduction . . .

DEIRDRE (*rises*). What!

CRONIN (*rises*). Listen, don't talk like a high class whore. It's a wonder you didn't say 'If you please, Mr Cronin ... what sort of a girl do you take me for?' (*To audience.*) Think I had better deliver a lecture – the art of seduction is an art or science every man or woman has to learn for himself. (*Arm around* DEIRDRE.) Be the very nature of the transaction it's a private transaction between you and me.

DEIRDRE (*rises*). How dare you!

CRONIN. I'm sorry. (DEIRDRE *sits down.*) I mean you and I. But I mean, who can you study in this business. Who have you ever seen seducing anyone? Up to now, I mean?

DEIRDRE. Well, there are very good scientific books written about it.

CRONIN. By God, if you want to die a virgin, you've got a sure shield for your virtue in that. Where's the poetry in that sort of literature?

He sings.

> 'Twas during my spasm, I had my orgasm,
> Coitus interruptitus,
> Old Kinsey, his report and all
> Old Kinsey, his report and all.

DEIRDRE (*to audience*). Kinsey is like Shaw. Shaw made our great grandparents and our grandparents so Shavian that they criticized him in the light of what he had taught them to accept as ordinary common sense. It's the same with Kinsey.

CRONIN. Kinsey! He was reassuring to everyone. When he announced for instance that ninety per cent of males had masturbated in their youth.

THE HERO. I never did.

CRONIN. You missed a damned good thing! But what can

scientists tell you about seduction. They go round parked cars with tape recorders. People don't always use the same ploy.

DEIRDRE. Might I ask which *ploy* you are *employing* at the moment.

CRONIN. Just now, I am the Cynical European Intellectual.

DEIRDRE. Do they shout at a girl . . . 'You have lovely eyes'?

CRONIN. Oh, no, that was my grandfather's line.

DEIRDRE. You mean you overheard him seduce your grandmother?

CRONIN. No, no, he was an actor and theatre manager. In a play called *A Royal Divorce* he acted Talleyrand, and seduced Josephine on the stage at the Queen's Theatre, Dublin.

DEIRDRE. That must have been a Passion Play.

CRONIN. That's very sharp. You are a witty and wonderful woman.

DEIRDRE. What ploy is that?

CRONIN. Manhattan Cocktail Party.

DEIRDRE. Were you in America?

CRONIN. No, thanks, that's for country people. I wouldn't like to do some poor bogman out of a job. [I might get a job interpreting.

DEIRDRE. Don't they speak English?

CRONIN. Of course they do and Irish too, but the trouble is they don't separate them.] Talking about the Passion Play, my grandfather used to leave the theatre dark during Holy Week. One year he hadn't been doing so well and couldn't really afford to close. All the other theatres were owned by Presbyterians and Jews. If he opened everyone would say the Presbyterians and Jews had more respect for Holy Week than he did.

DEIRDRE (*to audience*). He was on the horns of a dilemma.

CRONIN. Being on horns of any description wouldn't trouble my old granda, Jesus be just to him. But anyway, his brilliant son came to him and said, 'Father I know what we'll do.' 'Do

you now, Socrates,' said my grandfather, for he called his son
Socrates, and his daughter Sappho, because they acted
together as husband and wife in a play called 'When Greek
meets Greek' – she divorces him for being indifferent – real
classical drama. 'Well, what is it, Socrates?' 'We'll put on a
Passion Play for Holy Week.' 'Did you want to get us burned
at the stake? or summonsed or something.' 'You must not
know what a Passion Play is,' said my uncle Socrates. 'I most
certainly do,' said my granda. 'It's all that Paris stuff. Wasn't
I acting in one of those A la Francay leg shows in the Wind-
mill Theatre in London.' 'It's not that kind of a Passion
Play,' said my Uncle Socrates, 'it's about the passion of Our
Lord.' 'The passion of Our Who?' said my grandfather in
horror. 'Now look here, Sock, my son, I've been forty years
in show business, but I will not stand for a blasphemy
of that nature apart from the fact that it would be illegal
not to say unprofitable.' 'Arrah, you don't know what
you are talking about – they have it out in Germany, in
Obberammergau and get thousands of people from all
over the world to go and pay into it.' They do to this very
day.

DEIRDRE. Obberammergau. Mother was there. Wonderful acting,
all amateurs.

CRONIN. That's right – ex-S S men mit beards. (*He continues his
story.*) So, my Uncle Socrates explains to my granda about
the Passion Play and he says, 'That's great – we'll do great
business with matinees for convents and colleges – only one
thing.' 'What's that?' asks my Uncle Socrates. 'What'll we
do with the Queen's Moonbeams?' These were the chorus
girls. They were usually employed in dance numbers that
you would not perform for convents or colleges. 'Ph, that's
all right,' said Uncle Socrates, 'they will dance in very little.'
'Well,' said my grandfather, 'they wear so little now, it's only
the Grace of God they're not all dead from pneumonia, but
can we get away with it?' 'Certainly,' says my Uncle Socrates.

'Isn't it a class of a religious sermon against the Pharisees that crucified Christ.' 'Satisfyingly dramatic. Well, O.K.,' says my grandfather. 'But you won't forget to put in a plug for me ould friend Willie Rourke, the Baker, he puts his ad on the Fire Curtain?' 'Rourke, the Baker, will have his plug,' said my uncle, 'and in a place in the drama where all shall know it.' And so he had, for at the Last Supper, when Saint Peter passes Our Lord the wine and bread, he says, 'Take this and eat – it's Rourke's bread, fresh and crusty.'

CRONIN *starts to seduce* DEIRDRE.

DEIRDRE. I don't believe you are blind at all!

CRONIN (*takes off his glasses*). Well, no. (*Puts glasses away.*) I am not, thank God. (*He puts his arms round her a little more.*)

DEIRDRE (*tries to push him away.*) And maybe your friend is not blind either?

THE HERO (*beside them on tomb*). Aaaa-hh.

CRONIN. He is, the poor man, *and* deaf *and* dumb! (*Groan from* THE HERO.) Would you come to the seaside with me?

DEIRDRE. Why should I go with you?

CRONIN. Why the hell shouldn't you? Going round with your mother in a condition well-nigh bordering on incestuous lesbianism.

THE HERO (*aside*). I thought we would come to that!

DEIRDRE (*struggles wildly*). Let me go! (*Pants.*) Let me . . . let me go!

THE HERO. Ur-ur-ur-urrhh!

CRONIN (*to* THE HERO). Oh, shut up you, for Jesus' sake. Run away and shoot a Blueshirt or do something of a political or a religious nature.

DEIRDRE. You must be mad!

CRONIN. I am mad . . . mad with the villainy as the saying has it. We had to start somewhere. It'll get better as it goes on.

DEIRDRE. What makes you think it will go on? The-the-the . . .

CRONIN. Go on, say it. 'The cheek of you', you'ld say it only you know that's what factory girls say.

DEIRDRE. I don't know you.

CRONIN. You do know me. Your mother introduced us. And I told you about myself.

DEIRDRE. Yes, that you are a married man with a family.

CRONIN. Well, there you are. You know all about me, and I know nothing about you – I don't even know if you are a virgin.

DEIRDRE. How dare you! You . . . you . . . you!

CRONIN. Well, if you are *not* it's a sin against God, and if you *are* it's a sin against man. The sin against man is more important because we see God so seldom. However, if I can remedy the other. (*He raises his hand.*) 'If any nice girls shall come among you, I will fix them up.' (*He puts his hand on her shoulder and speaks easily.*) There, there. All this old chat of mine is a means of covering my shyness. We'll talk lovingly when you get to know me better.

DEIRDRE (*vigorously*). Why the hell do you think I should want to know you better. If my Uncle got a hold of you, he'd kick your arse for you!

CRONIN (*shocked*). What class of language do you call that, for a young lady? Your uncle can't do much to anyone. Your Ma has scattered his ashes.

DEIRDRE. My other uncle – The Hero Hogan. He fought Fascism in Spain.

CRONIN. Your family has a foot in every camp. Out tormenting and robbing the blacks in the Congo and fighting with the Reds in Spain. Bisexuals!

THE HERO (*grins*). Oooooohhh.

CRONIN. Here, you, for Jesus' sake, shut up.

DEIRDRE. Well, it's a cause of dissension at home. My mother is proud of the Belgian Count and her income comes from the Congo. And the Hero disapproves of living off the blood and sweat of the blacks.

THE HERO (*groans louder*). Ooohhhhhh!

CRONIN (*turns to him*). Here. (*Rises – takes* THE HERO *above tomb to tombs.*) For Jesus' sake, what's the matter with you? I'll shift him to another tombstone. (*Stands.*) Come on, get to hell out of here. (*He pulls* THE HERO *away and comes back without him.*) Can't have him there all day beside us, making the place gloomy with his groaning.

DEIRDRE. Maybe it's the only noise he can make, the poor man. He's a human being – I pity anyone suffering.

CRONIN. I'm a human being too. Pity is *my* vice and my downfall. I pity every sort and size of sinner even the ones who don't fall into any officially approved catogory of pityees. I've become one myself. I stand by the damned anywhere – if there are people put out of heaven put me out with them.

DEIRDRE. Even to hell?

CRONIN. Sure, it can't be much worse than Liverpool Prison. But just now – (*Puts his arm around her.*) You should pity me, and not be asking me why you should know me better.

DEIRDRE. Well, why should I know you better? What have you to offer a girl?

CRONIN. Don't ask me to show you. Do you want to get me arrested? The important thing is not what I should get but what I should give.

DEIRDRE. Who says that?

CRONIN. They always say that in Trade Union cases, to electricians and bricklayers. (*Pause.*) You have a lovely figure.

DEIRDRE (*she pulls his hand out from the neck of her blouse*). My figure has nothing to do with you!

CRONIN. A cat can look at a Queen!

DEIRDRE. And the Queen can kick his arse.

CRONIN. I don't know where you pick up such language.

DEIRDRE (*indignantly*). Do you take me for an ignoramus? I know about queers and everything.

CRONIN (*hugs her*). Then don't tell me you were never kissed before?

DEIRDRE (*pauses*). Well, not be a married man.

CRONIN. A married man is the only one you should ever let kiss you.

THE HERO (*from his tombstone across the stage*). Oooohhh.

CRONIN. Before a man has lived a couple of years with a woman, he is either timid or terrible.

DEIRDRE. And what about the girl that marries him?

CRONIN. Isn't she untrained except she is a widow?

DEIRDRE. Well, I am not a widow, so you'd better go back to your wife.

CRONIN. It's an education I'm offering you. I could make you a graduate, so to speak. You could do a P.H.D.!

DEIRDRE. What do you know about education?

CRONIN. Nothing, I suppose. [I never went to school much. (*To audience.*) Only to the Christian Brothers and that's education in reverse. It makes you very anti-clerical. For that reason, you could say the Christian Brothers are an enlightening influence in Ireland.] (*Sighs.*) I was never at a university. The only degree I ever got was the Third Degree. (*He is almost about to cry.*) But I have the natural grace of a simple Irish Catholic boy. Won't you be kind to me, Deirdre? Just as if I were a Spaniard or a Frenchman, instead of a poor Irishman, twisted for life on the cross of an Irishman's education, in a monastery?

DEIRDRE. Oh, surely there are worse things than an Irishman's education in a monastery?

CRONIN. Well, yes, an Irish *woman*'s education in a nunnery!

DEIRDRE. You are clever and witty. (*Throwing her arms around him.*) Oh!

CRONIN (*brightens up immediately and is his usual self*). Oh, you are a smasher, Deirdre. Oh, thanks, I accept that. (*He tries to manoeuvre his hand on her knee.*)

DEIRDRE. Ah, yes, but wait now. Just because I said – I don't want –

CRONIN. Well, what harm are we doing here? My wife wouldn't

begrudge me a bit of your kind attention, if that's troubling your conscience. She has a very sweet nature, my wife has.

DEIRDRE. You don't think I might resent you giving her a bit of your attention, if I let you . . .

CRONIN. Hurray. Me life on you. I'll get the mattress. (*He embraces her.*)

DEIRDRE (*struggles wildly*). Let me go! Let me go . . . you can't . . . I won't . . .

She breaks from him and gives him a resounding slap in the face.

THE HERO (*moans in great excitement*). Oooooooh (*In the manner of Harry Secombe.*) Urururururururururururur!

CRONIN (*to* THE HERO). Oh, kip in, for Jesus' sake. (*To* DEIRDRE.) Oh. (*Rubs his face.*) You've hurt me. (*He cries.*) And now you're going away and leaving me – with no one – no one to hug or kiss.

DEIRDRE (*stands and points at* THE HERO). You won't be all alone. There's your friend there.

CRONIN (*reasonably*). I am a broadminded man, but there's limits. (*He is cast down, his body bowed in despair.*) I suppose (*sadly*) I lack technique. I don't understand women. But where would I learn anything. (*Rises.*) Five years with the Irish Christian Brothers – nearly as bad as Eton or Harrow. (*He cries.*)

DEIRDRE. I'm off. (*She strides off.*)

CRONIN. Goodbye, Deirdre.

THE HERO (*looks after her and then comes menacingly to* CRONIN *and stands before him threateningly*). Urururururururur!

CRONIN (*looks up at him*). Oh, (*wearily*) you can give over your deaf and dumb language for now. She is gone. There is nobody to hear you.

THE HERO. What do you mean by trying to press your attentions on an innocent girl?

CRONIN. Innocent! (*Scornfully.*) Would you expect she'd know about queers?

THE HERO. She wasn't brought up in America!

CRONIN (*with interest*). Don't they have them there?

THE HERO. Only in the police force and on the Senate. They are not permitted in the Armed Forces. They have a regulation called Section Eight, which doesn't permit these people to be conscripted even in time of war. Pity they haven't got it in other armies. There'd be no more war!

THE HERO (*rises and sings*).

> The child that I carry will have to be
> laid on the steps of a nunnery,
> The man I call my own,
> Has turned funny and screams like
> a queen for cologne.

> His nails are all polished and in his hair,
> He wears a gardenia when I'm not there,
> Instead of flittin' he sits knittin'
> for a sailor he met in Thames Ditton.
> I must find another, for he loves me
> brother, not me (*exit*).

CRONIN (*sitting, addressing the audience*). My wife tries to cheer me up by saying that girls like me – that she loves me. But then she is my wife. I mean, I don't mean that she just loves me because a wife is supposed to love her husband. Ah no! My wife is a very, very, exceptional person, and she is very kind to everyone, and particularly to me.

But I'll tell you something for nothing. There's a lot of nonsense given out by the English and Americans about our attitude to women. They say it just to flatter themselves. Some old Jesuit in America attacks the Irish for not screwing early and often enough. A hundred years ago screwing and having kids was out of fashion and Paddy was being lambasted because he got married too soon, and had too many kids. It's like saying all Jews are capitalists because Rothschild is a capitalist, and all Jews are Reds because Karl Marx was a Jew – if they don't get you one way they get you another. If they don't get you by the beard they get you by the balls.

The English and Americans dislike only *some* Irish – the same Irish that the Irish themselves detest, Irish writers – the ones that *think*. But then they hate their own people who think. I just like to think, and in this city I'm hated and despised. They give me beer, because I can say things that I remember from my thoughts – not everything, because, by Jesus, they'd crucify you, and you have to remember that when you're drunk, but some things, enough to flatter them.

The great majority of Irish people believe that if you become a priest or a nun, you've a better chance of going to heaven. If it's a virtue to meditate in a monastery and get food and shelter for doing it – why then isn't it a virtue outside. I'm a lay contemplative – that's what I am.

CRONIN's *repose is abruptly shattered by a most piercing shriek from* DEIRDRE. *She comes running from the chapel and throws herself into* CRONIN's *arms.*

DEIRDRE (*in his arms*). Ooooohhhh.
CRONIN. There, there, my darling, I'll fetch the mattress.

THE HERO *comes rushing in.*

THE HERO. Where are they? The Fascist scum, where are they?
CRONIN (*points behind him with his thumb*). They went thataway. You're a brave man. See you find and destroy them – I'll look after your cousin, while you're on active service. Run

along – to the attack – she'll be in good hands – you can rely on me.

THE HERO. Thank you. (*He charges off.*)

PRINCE (*rushes on*). Someone has been tampering with my coffin!

THE HERO (*shouts from off*). Over here!

CRONIN. Thataway! (*Points with his thumb in opposite direction taken by* THE HERO. BONNIE PRINCE CHARLIE *rushes off.*)

DEIRDRE (*shivers and sobs*). Oh, I saw that old man in the coffin. It was awful.

CRONIN. Oh, come, come, he didn't look as bad as all that.

DEIRDRE. I'll stay here with you a while.

CRONIN. Certainly, I'll fetch the mattress. I mean, we might as well be comfortable. (*He rushes off and fetches a foam rubber mattress.*) Stand up a minute. (DEIRDRE *stands and he lays the mattress on the tomb.*) Now, you can lie down, I mean, sit down.

DEIRDRE (*hesitates*). I . . . I . . .

CRONIN. Sit down, for the love of Jesus, and I'll mind you. Please, Deirdre, come close to me and let us warm each other . . . (*She comes close to him.*) We are on a rapidly cooling planet.

DEIRDRE (*suddenly breaks from him and sits erect*). What ploy is this?

CRONIN. Science fiction. I'm a great reader, you know. (*Sighs.*) Ah, lie back, and we'll say nothing only. (*He sighs.*) Yes . . . yes . . . yes . . .

DEIRDRE. Yes. . . . Yes. . . . Yes. . . .

Blackout.

CRONIN (*a spot comes upon him*). When the author wrote this you weren't allowed to do it on a stage.

The spot goes out and all is black again.

DEIRDRE (*as full lights come on again*). But audiences have seen so much of it now they're bored with it.

CRONIN. I'll sing a song and *you* (*to audience*) can use your
imaginations, in the interval. (*Rises*.)

He sings.

> Oh, I met my love in a graveyard,
> We courted there 'cos we'd no bed
> And oh, happy love and embraces,
> We did it to cheer up the dead,
> I held her so close to a statue,
> We met at the door of a vault,
> And I whispered 'My dear, I'll be at you,
> And freely admit it's my fault'.

Chorus – the singing group have come back.

> It's my old Irish tomb,
> I'll be in there soon,
> But first you must kiss me,
> Beneath the harvest moon,
> No matter where you come from,
> No matter where you be,
> Remember your old Irish graveyard,
> And Father and Mother Machree.

> The day owl would hoot in the morning,
> The night owl would hoot in the night,
> With my horn in my hand, I'll be calling,
> My darling to join in the rite
> Of kissing and hugging, and feeling
> So cold on the top of the grave,
> I'd fall down before her and kneeling
> (*He kneels and holds out his hands*)
> I'd sing her this sweet serenade.

Chorus.

> It's my old Irish tomb,
> I'll be in there soon,
> But first you must kiss me,
> Beneath the harvest moon,
> No matter where you come from,
> No matter where you be,
> Remember that old Irish graveyard,
> And Father and Mother Machree.

Curtain.

Act Two

Act Two opens with DEIRDRE *and* CRONIN *on mattress.* THE HERO *enters with* BONNIE PRINCE CHARLIE.

THE HERO. Now! Now! What have you been doing on that mattress with my cousin.

CRONIN. We've just been getting to know one another. There's no crime in that!

THE HERO. No, I suppose you're right there. They make everything a crime these days. (*Sings.*)

> You'd think 'twas a crime to be human,
> To sometimes get scared in the park,
> When a copper sneaks up there behind you,
> And flashes his light in the dark.
>
> To regard savage dogs with suspicion,
> In case that the bastards would bite,
> To be hauled off to jail on suspicion,
> And scared of a scream in the night.
>
> You'd think 'twas a crime to be human,
> With sex education in bed,
> And postpone your thoughts of hereafter,
> 'Till after you are twenty years dead.
>
> To work overtime with young Nancy,
> And give her a coffee and roll,
> And likewise whatever she'd fancy,
> By weight or the lump or the whole.
>
> You'd think 'twas a crime to be human,
> And go for a swim in the sea,

And dance with no clothes in the sunshine,
And drink foreign lager for tea.

To regard co-existence with favour,
And nuclear weapons with fear,
To want more return for less labour,
Fatter fish, cheaper chips, better beer.

Let the heroes all die for the people,
If that is what they want to do,
And we'll struggle on here without them,
I've concluded, now, frolics to you.

THE HERO *exits*. BONNIE PRINCE CHARLIE *has entered during song*.

CRONIN (*sits up*). Oh, hello there, Mr Prince Charlie. How is the Loved Ones?

PRINCE. As well as may be expected. It's a bit difficult spreading the Gospel in this country.

[BARNEY. That's right, boss.]

CRONIN. You could sing that if you had an air to it!

PRINCE. It was the same when my own people were trying to civilize you.

[BARNEY. That's right, boss.]

CRONIN. When your people were trying to civilize us?

PRINCE. Listen, buddy, get this straight. I'm not an American.

[BARNEY. That's right, boss.]

CRONIN. No?

PRINCE (*his accent becomes very British*). Actually, old man, I'm not an American. I'm a Britisher. Straight from Notting Hill.

[BARNEY. That's right, boss.]

PRINCE. Straight from Notting Hill. I know we British gave you Paddies a hard time in the old days, Cromwell and all that . . . but think of the many advantages you could have had by embracing our way of life. Cricket, early closing . . . you could all wear blazers.

CRONIN. Well, if you don't mind me asking you . . . why did you not stop in England where you could have all these advantages yourself?

PRINCE. An unhappy love affair with a lady of title was the cause of my exile.

[BARNEY. That's right, boss.]

PRINCE. Now may I oblige the company with my song?

CRONIN. By all means. This is a real musical cemetery.

PRINCE. That is as it should be. In our Mother Memorial Park in Los Angeles we had the pipes and drums of the fifty-first Highland Division for a Loved One.

[BARNEY. That's right, boss (*in a Scottish ascent*).]

CRONIN. Was he an old Highland soldier?

PRINCE. He was from Beverley Hills. He had an agency for Johnnie Walker.

[BARNEY. That's right, boss (*in a Californian accent*).]

CRONIN. But being from Notting Hill doesn't make you Scotch.

PRINCE. I'm as Scotch as the Duke of Edinburgh. We're both British subjects. I was exiled for the love of a lady.

[BARNEY. That's right, boss.]

PRINCE (*clears his throat and sings ... I'm Lady Chatterley's Lover to the tune of Land of Hope and Glory*).

> I'm Lady Chatterley's lover,
> A game keeper that's me,
> I love my pheasants and plover,
> But mostly I love Lady C. (e-e-e-)
> Evelyn Waugh's a pushover,
> He made Sebastian Flyte,
> I went to Calais from Dover,
> Escaping scandal by night.
>
> (*Repeat last two lines.*)
>
> I went third class with Lolita,
> In a great grim ship,

What on earth could be sweeter,
That taking of her gym slip,
Fun in a hammock's gymnastic,
The exercise is good for your knees,
I got caught in the elastic,
And sent out an SOS please (ple-e-eease)

(*Repeat last two lines.*)

I love Whistler's mother,
Michaelangelo's David, too,
I love Van Gogh's brother,
And how is your Auntie Sue-ue-ue
I love the girl on the cover,
I love the bird and the bees,
But I'm Lady Chatterley's lover,
She is the girl for me-e-e-e-e.

(*Repeat last two lines.*)

[BARNEY. That's *not* right, boss, she's my bird.]

PRINCE (*camp*). Come along, dear!

MRS CRONIN (*appears from behind the Celtic Cross. To* DEIRDRE).
Now, love, I've to take Mr Cronin home. Maybe Mr Right
won't be long in finding you and you'll have a nice husband
like mine for yourself. (*To* CRONIN.) Come along, you know
it's your night for playing with the baby.

CRONIN. My country is a psychiatric state and my wife is my
nurse. (*But he rises and goes to* MRS CRONIN.)

MRS CRONIN. That's right, dear, come along now, and mind the
tombstones. (*She starts to drag him off, stopping as the sound
of Spanish martial music is heard.*)

CRONIN. Wait, the Blueshirts must be coming. I can hear a

band, and I see those two fallen women coming back. (BAWD I *and* BAWD II *appear*.) I'll get the groaner back sitting beside me, so that everything will look as it was before.

THE HERO *has entered.* CRONIN *and* THE HERO *sit on tomb.*

BAWD I. That soup was the making of me. (*To* DEIRDRE.) Oh, are you here all the time? Your mother is gone home. (DEIRDRE *does not answer*).

BAWD II (*excited*). There's a procession of Blueshirts or something up there, and you never know what bit of work we might get. (*To* CRONIN.) We'd be like them Turkish women you were talking about. 'Love among the tombstones . . .' They say it's lucky. (*To* DEIRDRE.) Would you think so, miss?

DEIRDRE. I wouldn't know. I am going home to my mother. Goodbye.

BAWD II. Don't take any bad money.

BAWD I. You can't go now till the procession is gone past.

*There is the sound of music and some men wearing blue shirts march across the back of the stage.**

BAWD II (*seductively to the* BLUESHIRTS). Hello, there, pidgeon pie, any good in your mind?

THE BLUESHIRT. Get away out of that, you concubine.

BAWD II. How dare you speak like that to a lady, you poxy bastard. I'm no porcupine.

BAWD I (*anxious for trade*). Be silent, Rose of Lima. They were out in Spain.

BAWD II. They ought to go back there, and not be coming over here and filling the country with vermin.

BAWD I. They are from here, and only went to Spain, to fight in a war between the Communists and the Catholics.

BAWD II. I'd have known them for Communists anywhere, the dirty looking lot of blackguards.

* We used dummy heads behind the ground row in the first production. *A.S.*

BAWD I. They are not Communists.

BAWD II. I heard you the first time. I'd have known them for Communists. They have every appearance of it. Look down the ranks. (*She points right of stage.*) There's Rape Ryan. The biggest whoremaster from here to Jipputty. (*She points again.*) And nature O'Neill, another good thing. A sweet thing in a child's frock. Oh, a low lot, you'd know them for Communists. But they'll never do away with the morality of Ireland, we'll keep it ever pure, the Island of Saints, and for the like of them – the poxy lot of bastards and that's praising them.

BAWD I. But they are not the Communists. These men were out fighting the Communists. Yes, them men were wounded, shot and bayoneted for the love of Jesus.

BAWD II (*changing her tune*). And for the love of Jesus wouldn't you know it. (*She reappraises the troops.*) A fine body of men. You'd know they were good Catholics by the respectable look of them. A credit to their country, they are.

BAWD I. Yes, a credit to their Faith and Fatherland.

BAWD II (*she points*). There's Pious Power. The holiest man in Dublin.

BAWD I. He's a sanctified man.

BAWD II. It's in his countenance – he has a face like a madman's arse.

The BLUESHIRTS' *leader comes in and addresses his parade. We hear the* BLUESHIRTS *come to attention.*

BLUESHIRT LEADER. Now give the three shouts, Number One, Viva Franco.

BLUESHIRTS. *Viva Franco.*

LEADER. Arriba España.

BLUESHIRTS. Arriba España.

THE HERO (*shouts*). Long live the Republic. (*He tears off the beard and black glasses.*)

CRONIN (*beside him*). The Hero Hogan. (*He runs and gets* THE HERO's *portable pulpit.*)

BLUESHIRTS. The Hero Hogan – the Bolshevik.

DEIRDRE. The Hero! My uncle! (*She runs to his side and kisses him.*) Down with Fascism.

BLUESHIRTS. Up the Blueshirts.

BAWD I. That's right, boys.

BAWD II. Up the Blue Room.

THE HERO *mounts his platform with his red flag.* DEIRDRE *stands beside him.*

THE HERO. We have called this meeting as a protest against Fascism.

All (except BLUESHIRTS*) gather round.*

BLUESHIRTS. Get down, you Red bastard.

THE HERO. When I was on the slopes of University Hill, outside Madrid . . .

BLUESHIRT LEADER. When we were at Salamanca . . .

Another BLUESHIRT *pulls him off. They return with offensive weapons.*

BAWD II. Were you ever in Belfast?

CRONIN. No, but he was in them that was.

BLUESHIRTS (*advancing on* THE HERO). Get the bastard.

THE HERO *produces a revolver. The* BLUESHIRTS *withdraw. The others try to get into the chapel.* THE HERO *turns to the* BAWDS *with his gun.*

BAWDS I and II. Oh, Jesus, Mary and Joseph. (*They dodge behind* CRONIN.)

CRONIN. And anyone else you can think of.

DEIRDRE (*who has stayed*). Carry on with your speech.

THE HERO. A Chairde.* (CRONIN *and the others come out from*
    * Irish – pronounced 'akorja'.

cover and stand beside DEIRDRE *at the platform.*) **Comrades and citizens of the Irish Republic.**

BAWD II. You frightened the lovely men.

THE HERO. I see they have retreated.

BAWD I. Lovely brave men that fought the Communists. Down with Communism.

DEIRDRE. Death to Fascism. (*She produces placards 'Down With Fascism'. 'I Hates Bad Grammar', 'I.R.A. Against the Bomb' and 'Up Down' which she gives to* CRONIN *and the* BAWDS.)

BAWD II. Down with rheumatism.

CRONIN. I'm a supporter of a Gaelic-speaking Ireland.

DEIRDRE. You are a Fascist reactionary.

CRONIN. Well, I think I might work up to be. (*He has the 'Up Down' placard with Co. Down colours.*)

DEIRDRE. And how would you get on in a Gaelic-speaking Ireland. Nil focal Ghaeilig agat. Nil focal.

CRONIN (*holds up his hands*). Language! language!

DEIRDRE. What would you do in a Gaelic-speaking Ireland? Well?

CRONIN. Well, I could be a deaf mute. [And I could be Catholic Archbishop of Dublin . . . he doesn't know any Irish, but he's studying it through the medium of Gaeniclogy.]

THE HERO (*speaks from his chair platform*). Amid the thunder of guns and the crash of bombs, the brave soldiers of the proletariat stood shoulder to shoulder against the Fascist hyenas . . . (*ad lib.*)

A BLUESHIRT *rushes on the stage and clutches* BAWD II *by the arm.*

BLUESHIRT. Don't be listening to that aetheist. Come away with me. (*She goes with him.*) You there. (*He speaks to* THE HERO.) The Blueshirts will be back for you. (*They go off.*)

CRONIN. His taste must be in his mouth. And so must hers.

BAWD I. He was one of the men that was out fighting against the Communists in Spain.

CRONIN. He should get reduced rates, so.

BAWD I. What do you mean by that, you dirty low cur?

THE HERO. Now, now, do not insult the returned warrior.

He sings.

> Let loose my fierce crusaders,
> O'Duffy wildly cried,
> My grim and bold mosstroopers,
> That poached by Shannon side,
> Their shirts are blue, their backs are strong,
> They've cobwebs on the brain,
> And if Franco's moors are beaten down,
> My Irish troops remain.
>
> In old Dublin town my name is tarred,
> On pavement and slum wall.
> In thousands on her Christian Front
> The starving children call.
> But with my gallant ironsides,
> They call to us in vain,
> For we're off to slaughter workers in
> The sunny land of Spain.
>
> At Badajo's red ramparts,
> The Spanish workers died,
> O'Duffy's bellowing Animal Gang
> Sing hymns of hate with pride.
> The sleuths that called for Connolly's blood
> And Sean MacDiammuid's too,
> Are panting still for workers gone,
> From Spain to far Peru.
>
> Fall in! Fall in! O'Duffy cried,
> There's work in Spain to do,

A harp and crown we all will gain,
And shoot the toilers through,
In Paradise an Irish harp,
A Moor to dance a jig,
A traitor's hope, a hangman's rope,
An Irish peeler's pig.

BLUESHIRT (*off*). Get him.

BLUESHIRTS *enter menacingly with very offensive weapons.*

THE HERO. Now listen to me, you set of superannuated police
louts. (*Raises his voice.*) The Catholic Church in Spain ...
BLUESHIRT (*shouts*). Have respect for religion, you poxy bastard.

He raises a submachine gun. THE HERO *fires his revolver and they
retreat across the stage. One man is wounded and he drags himself
after them, all off.* BAWD II *runs back on the stage.*

BAWD II. Ooooh! He's shot ... he's wriggled with bullets. He's
wriggled.
CRONIN (*returning*). Quick, here. We must get away before the
peelers get here. (*Exits fast.*)

BAWD II *is left with* THE HERO *who has taken possession of submachine gun.*

BAWD II. Wait for me! Wait! (*She runs after them.*) Wait for me!
THE HERO (*to audience*). The Irish Republic was cradled in
revolutionary France.

Puts his hand on his breast and sings, to the air of The Marseillaise.

(1) The dogs of war let loose are howling,
      That treacherous kings consultant raise,

(2) The dogs of war let loose are howling,
(3) And low our fields and cities blaze.
    And shall we basely view the ruin,
(4) While lawless force with guilty stride,
    Spreads desolation far and wide,
    With crime and blood his hands embruing.
(5) To arms to arms ye brave,
    The patriot sword unsheathe,
    March on! March on!
    All hearts resolved,
    To liberty or death.

During song, the set changes to MRS MALLARKEY's *room.*

To reinforce certain lines of the song, various symbolic props are carried across the stage during the change :

(1) *1798 rebellion pikes.*

(2) *A British crown and a representation of King William of Orange.*

(3) *Fire effect.*

(4) *A British soldier in riot gear and a barbed wire fence representing Long Kesh Internment Camp.*

(5) *A coffin, carried shoulder high. It is draped with Irish Tricolour and Union Jack and covered with wreaths, etc. A muffled drum beats.*

The scene is the Living Room of a Victorian house furnished rather like the meeting hall of a small Protestant sect. There is a banner on the back wall reading 'To Hell with the Devil! God Save the

Queen'. There is a sofa in the centre of the stage. MRS MALLARKEY
is reading a speech.

MRS MALLARKEY. And, dear brothers and sisters, the modern
dance, with its intimate contact of bodies, especially now
when the scant clothing of young women leaves them so
slightly covered, is inevitably a source of serious sex excitement.

Enter DEIRDRE *and* CRONIN, *in excitement.*

DEIRDRE. Mammy! Mammy!
MRS MALLARKEY (*holds up her hand*). I am rehearsing my speech
for the Anti-Dancing Committee of the Female Prevention
Society. (*She turns to* CRONIN.) You are a man, sir. (*He nods.*)
CRONIN. Yes, ma'am.
MRS MALLARKEY. What is he doing here, Deirdre?
DEIRDRE. He is . . . He is . . . he is a friend of mine, Mammy.
MRS MALLARKEY. A friend of yours? A man? You have a man
for a friend, Deirdre? What is the meaning of this?
DEIRDRE. Well, Cronin is only . . .
MRS MALLARKEY. Only what? He is a man and that is sufficient
for me. I know men. My husband, your father, was a man.
(*To* CRONIN.) Are you a Roman Catholic?
CRONIN. Er, yes, ma'am.
MRS MALLARKEY. I'd have known by your little button nose, and
your slanty, slitty eyes. (*To* DEIRDRE.) Deirdre, how could
you sink to such evil. A man, and a Roman Catholic! (*To*
CRONIN.) This is a Christian house and we don't want
Roman Catholics here.
DEIRDRE. Our cousin is in serious trouble and Cronin must
remain here, with some other people for a little while.
MRS MALLARKEY. What kind of trouble?
DEIRDRE. He wants you to go downstairs and see him. It is
serious trouble.

MRS MALLARKEY. Oh, our poor dear cousin, though he is a
vessel of wrath, I must go to him. You may sit down.
(CRONIN *and* DEIRDRE *sit on the sofa beside each other.*) No,
at each end of the sofa, please. (*Exit* MRS MALLARKEY.
CRONIN *goes to embrace* DEIRDRE.)

DEIRDRE. Hold on! We must be practical. (*She places a chair
against the door.*)

CRONIN (*to audience*). I wasn't long about making her practical.

DEIRDRE. You mustn't mind her, Cronin. My mother is a brother.

CRONIN. Your mother is a brother?

DEIRDRE. I mean she is a Plymouth Brother. I mean a Plymouth
Sister. They are very strict.

CRONIN (*moves towards her*). I am glad you're not my sister (*and
closer*), and I'm glad you're not too strict. (*He moves up to
her corner and puts his arms round her. She eases herself and
rises.*)

DEIRDRE. Mummy thinks it's hell fire for a man to put his arms
round a girl.

CRONIN. I think it's very pleasant. Your father must have thought
so too. What did your mother think of your father, when he
was putting his arms round her. She must have put up with
it some time otherwise you wouldn't be here for me to put
my arms round you.

DEIRDRE. She loved Daddy, at the beginning all right. They
met in Merrion Hall at a Gospel Service, and they sang
'Fires of Hell Burn Brightly and the Screeches of the
Damned'.

CRONIN. Very romantic.

DEIRDRE. When I was two years' old he went to a circus. That
was sinful enough for one of the Brethren, but he fell in
love with a fire-swallower, and they ran away together. She
was a Roman Catholic fire-swallower.

CRONIN. Well, I'm a pint man myself.

DEIRDRE. Poor father met his end that way. This woman was
teaching him fire-swallowing and he had a fit of coughing

and swallowed the fire the wrong way. Mummy's never looked at another man since. Only the Hero.

CRONIN. It's a wonder they don't get married.

DEIRDRE. It's the Hero's politics. He was a Republican during the Trouble, and mother was on a Committee providing comforts for Black and Tans.

CRONIN. Hey, how about a little comfort for me?

MRS MALLARKEY (off). Deirdre, Deirdre.

DEIRDRE. I think mother is coming, darling. (*She rises and moves the chair back to its original position. They sit at opposite ends of the sofa.*)

CRONIN (*in an affected voice*). About the doctrine of total immersion. (*Enter MRS MALLARKEY.*) Ah, saved by the bell.

MRS MALLARKEY (*quickly to DEIRDRE*). I could get no sense from our cousin except that he is in frightful trouble and will be in worse trouble if I don't allow all these people to remain here. What is it all about, Deirdre?

THE HERO *enters followed by the* BAWDS, BONNIE PRINCE CHARLIE *and his friend.*

DEIRDRE. Oh, there was a bit of an upset at a Meeting we held.

THE HERO. This way, please, ladies.

MRS MALLARKEY. Here he is, with his followers. Cousin, what is this trouble. Why are these people here?

THE HERO (*confidentially to MRS MALLARKEY*). I have killed a man.

MRS MALLARKEY. I could have foretold it from years ago when you publicly associated with them Fenians. He that lives by the sword shall perish by the sword.

BAWD II. It wasn't a sword, ma'am . . . it was a gun.

BAWD I. And it wasn't your cousin that perished, it was the other poor bastard.

BAWD II. Wriggled with bullets, he was, I seen him.

THE HERO (*sotto voce, to MRS MALLARKEY*). They could identify me to the police. They must remain here till I prepare my defence.

MRS MALLARKEY (*sighs*). All right. (*To the people.*) You may sit down. I am reading my speech for the Anti-Dancing Committee of the Female Prevention Society. It will do them no harm to listen. (BAWD I *and* BAWD II, *etc.*, *sit down on chairs.* THE HERO *sits on the sofa between* DEIRDRE *and* CRONIN.) Hem! (MRS MALLARKEY *reads from her paper.*) 'The modern dance, with its intimate contact of bodies, is inevitably a source of serious sex excitement, especially now when the scant clothing of young women leaves them so slightly covered. (MRS MALLARKEY's *eye falls on the large expanse of bare leg showing beneath* BAWD II's *minute mini-skirt. Seeing* MRS MALLARKEY's *basilisk eye upon her,* BAWD II *ineffectually covers her legs with her handbag.*)

BAWD I. The dirty bitches.

BAWD II. That sex excitement is getting a terrible grip everywhere.

MRS MALLARKEY. 'In a study of dancing published some time ago thirty mature people were asked to say what they thought of it. Two of the group were experienced clergymen. And in the modern dance tunes there is unmistakable suggestiveness. A penny a kiss, a penny a hug.'

BAWD I. Cut price whores.

MRS MALLARKEY. 'Another is "My Resistance is Low" where virtue is vanquished because resistance is low.'

Her audience, led by THE HERO, *clap.*

BAWD I. Hear, hear, over there.

BAWD II. And now, what about a little drink?

MRS MALLARKEY. This is a godly house, madam, and I have never permitted intoxicants across its door.

BAWD II (*rises*). Then we must go where we can get some gargle. (*To* BAWD I.) Come along, Gemma Gal gani.

BAWD I (*rises*). Right, Magso.

THE HERO (*raises his hand*). No, no, good ladies, just a moment. (*In a lower tone to* MRS MALLARKEY.) We can't let them leave. They may go to the police immediately. Do you want to see me hanged.

MRS MALLARKEY. You may sit down again. My cousin will arrange for you to have some refreshments. The sin is his, not mine.

BAWD I. I don't give a curse whose it is as long as I get a jar.

THE HERO (*goes to the phone. Dials a number and speaks at the phone*). Hello! Hello! Mrs Mallarkey's here. Send up 3 bottles of whiskey and four dozen of stout. Yes, yes. (THE BAWDS *signal frantically*.) Ah yes, and a bottle of gin.

MRS MALLARKEY. Cousin.

THE HERO (*into phone*). Mrs Mallarkey will not partake. It is for her guests. Thank you.

He puts down phone.

CRONIN (*rises and goes to the phone*). I must ring up the Relieving Officer.

BAWD II. We give outdoor relief!

CRONIN. My wife and children haven't eaten for two days.

MRS MALLARKEY. How many children have you?

CRONIN. I have six.

MRS MALLARKEY. But you seem to me to be a very young man to have such a large family.

CRONIN. I am twenty-two, but I was married when I was seventeen.

MRS MALLARKEY. Six children at twenty-two, what a beautiful Roman Catholic family.

CRONIN. I am a Protestant.

MRS MALLARKEY. You are a sex maniac.

CRONIN. Well, it gives me a healthy appetite. (*To* THE HERO.) I wonder, would you knock up a sandwich to go with that beer?

THE HERO. I'm sure we could. (*To* DEIRDRE.) Deirdre will see to it – get some sandwiches, dear, for our guests.

MRS MALLARKEY. For *your* guests, cousin.

DEIRDRE. I'll go down to the kitchen and fix up something. Cronin, will you come and give me a hand?

MRS MALLARKEY. Deirdre! You cannot be alone in the kitchen with a man.

CRONIN. We'll all go down and help her. I'll carry up the drink.

BAWD II. And we'll carry up the sandwiches. (*Exit* DEIRDRE *and* CRONIN *followed by* BAWD I *and* BAWD II, BONNIE PRINCE CHARLIE [*and friend*].)

MRS MALLARKEY. Cousin, who are all these people?

THE HERO. I tell you they saw me shoot this man, and could go to the police and identify me. Do you want me to be hanged?

MRS MALLARKEY. Get along with you. There is no fear of you being hanged. It is more of your nonsense.

THE HERO. How do you know it is.

MRS MALLARKEY. It always is. Deirdre knows it, as well as I do. But how do you get mixed up with such sinful paupers.

THE HERO. They can't help being poor.

MRS MALLARKEY. Everyone can help being poor.

THE HERO. The Lord and His Family were poor.

MRS MALLARKEY. They were in humble, frugal circumstances, but they were not tramps. They had a little carpenter's shop and probably did a bit in the hardware line as well, like father.

Two faces appear at the window. They could be BLUESHIRTS.

THE HERO. Well, anyway, if these people go and identify me to the police it will certainly be very serious for me.

The faces disappear.

MRS MALLARKEY. Cousin (*rises*), I dream of that happy day when you will put on the white robe of sanctification. I will join you, and be your sponsor . . . A joyful reunion.

THE HERO. Your religion is a lethal one. The Pierrepoints were Plymouth Brethren and Haigh the acid bath murderer was a Plymouth Brother. It must have been a joyful reunion when they met on the gallows.

Enter BAWD I *and* BAWD II, CRONIN, DEIRDRE, BONNIE PRINCE CHARLIE [*and friend*].

CRONIN (*sings to* THE HERO *on sofa, unaccompanied.*

> 'Twas in the town of Wexford they
>   sentenced him to die,
> 'Twas in the town of Wexford they
>   built their gallows high . . .

MRS MALLARKEY. Stop that ridiculous song. Nobody is sentenced to die. Even if the man was shot. I expect it wasn't in a vital part of the body.

CRONIN. He was shot in the arse hole.

MRS MALLARKEY. Rectum, rectum.

CRONIN. Wrecked him . . . it near killed him.

BAWD I. Give us a song.

DEIRDRE. Recite us that piece you read at Aunt Mary's bedside.

MRS MALLARKEY. It was disgraceful to read such stuff at her dying bedside.

THE HERO. Well, it was an expensive bit of reading. It got me cut out of her Will.

MRS MALLARKEY. Filth! No wonder.

THE HERO. It was not filth. It was from the Rambler by Doctor Samuel Johnson: 'It is well remembered here, that about seven years ago, a boy named Frolick, a tall boy with lank hair, was remarkable for stealing eggs and sucking them . . .' It was not my fault that old printers spelt 'sucking' with an 'f'.

MRS MALLARKEY. To a dying woman you read this filth.

THE HERO. 'Stealing eggs and sucking them'?

MRS MALLARKEY. Away and suck yourself.

THE HERO. That would be a moral wrong and a physical impos-
sibility.

MRS MALLARKEY (*holding up a bottle of Martini*). Is this non-
intoxicating?

THE HERO (*impatiently*). Yes, yes, yes.

BAWD I. Now, now, birds in their little nests agree.

BAWD II (*her speech a little slurred from drink*). And tish a shameful
shight . . .

BAWD I. When children of one family fall out and bark and bite.

BAWD II. Let's have a bar of a song. Teresa Avila, give us a song.

BAWD I. I don't mind. Give me a big chord, please.

*Two musicians dressed as gas meter collectors enter unobtrusively
and accompany the song.*

BAWD I *sings*.

> I am a decent married woman, Biddy Reilly is my name.
> I married a hurdygurdy man, below in Chancery Lane.
> But now he's gone and left me, to sail across the sea,
> And since I'm left here all alone, I'm out upon the spree.

> (*Chorus.*)

> Ah, there goes Biddy Reilly and she's taking to the sup,
> There goes Biddy Reilly and she'll never give it up.
> First she goes off to the pop, then she's sure to have a
> drop,
> The Heart of the Rowl is Biddy Reilly.

> There's Mrs Doyle in Number Nine, she is a big bow
> vow,
> She goes around from lobby to lobby, and causes many
> a row,

She spoke of me the other day to my neighbour Mat
McGee,
But I hope she picks on Reilly when she's out upon the
spree.

(*Repeat Chorus.*)

*General applause with remarks of 'Good on you', 'A lovely song'
and from* MRS MALLARKEY '*Most creditable I'm sure*'.

There is a sudden silence. We hear the clock ticking. First MRS
MALLARKEY, *then everyone else realizes that there are strangers
present and turn to look at them. When they realize they are the
centre of attention they empty the gas meter, note the reading, raise
their hats and exit. We notice that they very closely resemble the*
BLUESHIRTS.

BAWD II. Maria Concepta has a heart of gold, though she is poor
and sinful.
MRS MALLARKEY. I have a heart of gold, but I'm not poor and
sinful. My cousin is an atheist.
THE HERO. Only in daylight. When it gets dark, I get frightened
and religious, and when I'm ill. Just now I am in good health
and it is not dark.

*Again, the musicians enter. This time they are as electricity board
men.*

He sings.

Oh, tra, la la la la; Oh, tra la la la la
An honest God's the noblest work of man.
But keep your distance from him if you can,
By plane or ship, avoid his grip,
It is the safest plan,
An honest God's the noblest work of man.

Oh, tra la la la la la la,
He caught them all, no matter how they ran,
Though they'd resigned from his immortal plan,
Twas all the same, once in the game,
You can't throw in your hand,
An honest God's the noblest work of man.

BAWD I. Hurrah, Up God.
BAWD II. An Phoblact Abu – Long Live the Republic.

The same rigmarole this time reading the electric meter with a torch.

DEIRDRE. I think it's time for mother's committee meeting.
CRONIN. So it is.
THE HERO. Let us assemble.

They move in their chairs.

MRS MALLARKEY. Dear Deirdre, it is very good of you to remember that this is my committee meeting night. (*To all.*) The doctor said I was to have my committee meeting at least once a week. Ahem!
BAWD I. You too.
MRS MALLARKEY. Our observations and reports tell us that sex is once more getting under way in this fair isle of ours. Nude bathing, mixed marriages and free love.
BAWD I. Disgraceful.
BAWD II. Scabbing the job.
BAWD I. We don't mind fair competition: but free love!
BAWD II. And Immaculate Contraception.
BAWD I. Deny it who can.
MRS MALLARKEY. I've not finished. (*Resumes her speech.*) The present day is a time of selfishness. People seek pleasure and comfort in this world. They are frightened of the next. Even the Salvation Army is full of perverts.
CRONIN. I don't believe that. I know some is married with families.

MRS MALLARKEY. Perhaps you don't know what a pervert is.

CRONIN. Of course I do. I read biographies.

BAWD I. A pervert is when a Catholic becomes a Protestant.

THE HERO. Not a pervert. A convert.

BAWD I. A convert is when a Protestant becomes a Catholic.

THE HERO. In England a pervert is a man who has sex relations
with other men.

CRONIN. Well, I might have a go at that too. A change is as good
as a rest. A Catholic convert pervert that's me. (*Stands and
clutches his crotch and says in a feminine voice.*) I've got
retractable undercarriage. (*Sings soprano.*) 'When I was a
maiden, fair and young, on the pleasant banks of Lee ...'
(*He puts his arm round* DEIRDRE.)

MRS MALLARKEY. Think of your wife, sir.

CRONIN. I tried my luck with her as any young fellow will. I'd
have been happy enough, passing my time with masturbation
and Rugby football, like any other decent Christian boy, but
her mother encouraged her.

MRS MALLARKEY. Her mother encouraged her to er let you er.

CRONIN. Yes, to let me er, and I did er as often as possible. I
wasn't got in a foundry. Her mother said to her, to let me
er. 'Go on,' says she, 'let him, the father has plenty of money
and a good business.'

MRS MALLARKEY. Your father is a wealthy man?

CRONIN. He was but he was ruined by hygiene.

MRS MALLARKEY. By hygiene? (*She glances at the bottle she has
been swigging from. It is evident that it is far from being non-
intoxicating.*) Martini and Rossi. By Appointment to Her
Majesty the Queen.

CRONIN. Ruined by hygiene: he used to supply sawdust to public
houses. Now, the days of the big spitters is over.

BAWD II. Anyway, up the Salvation Army.

THE HERO. That's what all perverts say.

            'They sold their souls for penny rolls,
            cold beef and belly bacon.'

CRONIN. I never got neither cold beef nor hot beef in the Salvation Army.

BAWD I. I'm sure he never sold his soul in the Salvation Army . . . Though I preached at the mercy seat one time. (*Stands at table.*) Brethren and Sisthren. (*All shout 'Alleluia' as at a revival meeting of the hot gospel variety.*) Yesterday, I was a common prostitute.

BAWD II. A desthitute prosthitute.

BAWD I. A destitute prostitute . . . I'll start all over again. Brethren and Sisthren.

ALL. Alleluia!

BAWD I. Yesterday I was a common prostitute, a destitute prostitute upon the streets of Dublin.

PRINCE. Wash my sins in the blood of the lamb, till my soul is white as snow.

[BARNEY. That's right, boss.]

BAWD I. I was weak, weak with the weight of me sins, pressing down upon me poor bent, bowed shoulders.

ALL. Lord! Lord!

BAWD I. Lord save us! But now (*exultantly*) I am so happy in the faith of my Lord, Saviour . . .

ALL. Alleluia!

BAWD II. That's right, Our Shavuour, he will shave us, shampoo us and hair cut us.

BAWD I. But now, I am so happy, in the faith of my Lord, Saviour and Deliverer.

ALL. Alleluia!

BAWD I. That I could put my foot through the bleeding drum . . .

Cheers.

BAWD II. Hip, hip, hurray.

CRONIN. Where's Deirdre?

THE HERO. She's around behind.

CRONIN. I know she has, but where is she?

DEIRDRE. I'm here, Cronin.

CRONIN. Come here and sit on me knee.

MRS MALLARKEY. I don't know whether she should or not. You are a married man. (DEIRDRE *comes and sits down beside him.*)

CRONIN. I was only married in the Protestant Church. That doesn't count.

MRS MALLARKEY. Fetch your harp, Deirdre.

DEIRDRE. Would you like to hear me play? I'll get the harp.

MRS MALLARKEY. She should really be wearing her Gaelic costume.

CRONIN. I don't mind if she plays in her skin.

MRS MALLARKEY. Think of your wife, sir 'in her skin'.

CRONIN. I often think of my wife 'in her skin'.

BAWD II. I'll sing a song [myself while she's getting her harp.] I am a soprana.

This time the musicians appear as dustmen.

BAWD I. She is too.

BAWD II (*sings*).

> She combed her hair, and she combed her
>   hair,
> She combed her hair, and she combed her
>   hair.
> She combed her hair, and she combed her
>   hair,
> She combed her hair, and she combed her
>   hair.

BAWD I. Hear, hear over there. That was beautiful, Rose of Lima.

MRS MALLARKEY. It was very well rendered.

CRONIN. You must give me the words of that some time.

Again the rigmarole. The musicians on this occasion go off with the dustbin.

BAWD I. Of course she took prizes for music and electricution at the College.

THE HERO. Oh, your friend was at College?

BAWD II. The Mary Magdaleen Home for Repentent Prostitutes.

BAWD I (*getting a tray of sherry in delicate glasses and handing them round*). We do call it the College. Young girls that's only new to the business, they learn the ropes. Some of them was only doing it for fun like, when they were brought into the College . . . well, the whores there, they teach them to get a few shillings for themselves, then they go over to London and make a career by hard work and honest toil.

BAWD II. Yes, I even heard of a girl got a job in Hollywood acting a whore on the pictures. A Roman whore, like. It was very athletic, she had to be flung naked over a cliff into a pit, to roaring beasts. There was a hundred of them.

MRS MALLARKEY. A hundred naked harlots.

BAWD II. And a hundred roaring beasts. Every roaring beast got a naked whore.

BAWD I. And wasn't she appearing before the High Priests of the Pagan Temple.

BAWD II. The film was all the Bible, you know. Naked whores, and pagan priests and roaring beasts. Really holy, it was.

BAWD I. I don't think it would be right to appear naked before pagan priests. I wouldn't mind our own like or even a Minister or a Rabbi, but I'd draw the line at appearing naked before a pagan, it'd be against me theology.

MRS MALLARKEY. I do not think in Ireland you would get many offers of that sort from a clergyman of any denomination.

BAWD II. Oh, no matter what their abomination, none of them got it for stirring their tea with. What does a bishop like better than a good conenderum?

MRS MALLARKEY. I'm afraid I don't know.

BAWD II. A good nun under him!

BAWD I. Rose of Lima. Conjugate yourself to a near resemblance of respectability.

[DEIRDRE *returns with an imaginary harp.*

MRS MALLARKEY. Now, order for the performer.

DEIRDRE *bends forward over her imaginary harp and goes through the motions of playing.*
Long pause.

BAWD I. What are you going to play?
BAWD II. Play a game of pontoon.

Pause.

THE HERO. Most moving, these old Irish airs.
BAWD I. Which one is she going to play?
MRS MALLARKEY. Sh, sh, 'I am asleep and do not waken me' she is playing. This is the second verse.
THE HERO (*murmurs*). Wonderful. How Sam Beckett would have loved this. 'I am asleep and do not waken me.'
BAWD II. Me too.

Snores gently and indeed they are all nearly asleep. DEIRDRE *finishes and drapes herself over her instrument.*

DEIRDRE (*murmurs*). There.

Applause.

MRS MALLARKEY. My dear, you excelled yourself.
THE HERO. Ah, it wrung my heart.
BAWD I. Ah, silence is golden.
CRONIN. The Marx Brothers have a sister.]

There is a loud banging on the outside door.

GARDA. Open up there, Garda Siochana* on duty.
   * Police.

SERGEANT. Open up there.

BAWD I. Holy God, it's the guards.

MRS MALLARKEY. How dare they, the dirty Fenians? Disturbing a decent Protestant house – tell them to go away, Deirdre.

DEIRDRE. I certainly will, mother.

DEIRDRE *exits.*

THE HERO. Now will you believe me. They have come to arrest me. Where can I hide?

BAWD I. Stuff yourself under the antimacassar.

BAWD II. Watch your language, Maria. The guards is here.

Enter MRS CRONIN (*with tray*), DEIRDRE, *two policemen, one a sergeant. They have the same faces as the* BLUESHIRTS, *the gas metermen, the electricity metermen and the dustmen.*

MRS CRONIN (*going to* CRONIN). Here's your tea.

CRONIN. You're after leading the guards here. They're after the Hero.

SERGEANT. Now thin, fwats going on here.

GARDA. Looks like an immoral orgy, Sergeant. These women are street walkers.

BAWD II. Well, we don't waste the taxpayers' money riding around in dirty big foreign made squadcars.

THE HERO *is trying to get out of the window. He drops his violin case and the tommy gun falls out.*

SERGEANT. Look out, Mick! That man is armed!

GARDA (*producing revolver*). Put up your hands and come back in here.

DEIRDRE (*leaping at guard*). You leave my uncle alone, you bullying bastard.

The revolver goes off, killing CRONIN.

CRONIN *staggers and collapses dead in the centre of the stage. The lights go dim and the rest of the cast freeze while a few bars of the traditional lament, 'Anach Chuain', are played on a tin whistle. Then the ladies of the cast join in singing the lament as they and the men group themselves round the corpse.*

> Annsúd Dia h-Aoine chluinfea an caoineadh
> Ag teacht gach taoidh, agus greadadh bos,
> A's a lán, tar oidhche trom tuirseach claoidhte
> Gan ceó le deanamh aca acht A' síneadh corp.
>
> A Dhia 's a Chríosta D'fhulaing iodhbairt
> Do cheannuigh (go) fírinneach an bocht 's on nocht.
> Go parrthas naomh tha go dtugtair saor leadt
> Gach (creatuir) diobh da'r thuit faoi an lot.

When the body is concealed from the audience by the cast a dummy is substituted for the actor playing CRONIN, *who moves upstage, still unseen by the audience. Simultaneously the coffin which has been left conveniently in the wings is wheeled in to a position up centre. If there's a lift available the coffin should be placed immediately down stage of it (if necessary the table used by* MRS MALLARKEY *may be struck or moved aside to allow for the positioning of the coffin).*
Also at this point the bunting piece which also holds the picture of Elizabeth II should be flown out and MRS MALLARKEY's *room walls moved off stage somewhat so that some parts of the cemetery set will be revealed when the lights are raised on them.*
CRONIN *appears leaning over upstage of the coffin (which is covered in flowers and wreaths at the opening of the play).*

CRONIN. O Pog na hone, I'm all alone. The darkness here would blind you. But with the state the world is in you'll not be long behind me. The grave's a dark and silent place and none there are to there embrace.

DEIRDRE *and* MRS CRONIN *are either side of him.*

PRINCE. This is pure plagiarism.
CRONIN. Barefaced robbery. Talent borrows, genius robs.
     Go easy with your nuclear experiments or you might join
     me sooner than you expect. Slan leat anois. See you soon,
     I hope.
CRONIN *turns and slowly walks up stage into the mist.*

The men sing softly to the audience.

> It's my old Irish tomb
> I'll be in there soon
> But first you must kiss me
> Beneath the harvest moon
> No matter where you come from
> No matter where you be
> Remember your old Irish graveyard
> And a stone marked R.I.P.

*As the song is being sung, a collage-type drop framework comes in
and the actor playing* CRONIN *is raised (on a lift or on flying wires)
high enough to be nearly totally visible behind the coffin forming a
tableau rather like the sort of religious kitsch frequently seen on the
front of a mass card.*

CRONIN *sings the last line of new version of 'Old Irish Tomb' solo
as the curtain falls.*

Methuen's Modern Plays

EDITED BY JOHN CULLEN AND GEOFFREY STRACHAN

Paul Ableman	*Green Julia*
Jean Anouilh	*Antigone*
	Becket
	Poor Bitos
	Ring Round the Moon
	The Lark
	The Rehearsal
	The Fighting Cock
	Dear Antoine
John Arden	*Serjeant Musgrave's Dance*
	The Workhouse Donkey
	Armstrong's Last Goodnight
	Left-handed Liberty
	Soldier, Soldier and other plays
	Two Autobiographical Plays
John Arden and Margaretta d'Arcy	*The Business of Good Government*
	The Royal Pardon
	The Hero Rises Up
Ayckbourn, Bowen, Brook, Campton, Melly, Owen, Pinter, Saunders, Weldon	*Mixed Doubles*
Brendan Behan	*The Quare Fellow*
	The Hostage
Barry Bermange	*No Quarter* and *The Interview*
Edward Bond	*Saved*
	Narrow Road to the Deep North
	The Pope's Wedding
	Lear
John Bowen	*Little Boxes*
	The Disorderly Women

Bertolt Brecht	*Mother Courage*
	The Caucasian Chalk Circle
	The Good Person of Szechwan
	The Life of Galileo
	The Threepenny Opera
Syd Cheatle	*Straight Up*
Shelagh Delaney	*A Taste of Honey*
	The Lion in Love
Max Frisch	*The Fire Raisers*
	Andorra
Jean Giraudoux	*Tiger at the Gates*
Simon Gray	*Spoiled*
	Butley
Peter Handke	*Offending the Audience* and
	Self-Accusation
	Kaspar
Rolf Hochhuth	*The Representative*
Heinar Kipphardt	*In the Matter of J. Robert Oppenheimer*
Arthur Kopit	*Chamber Music and other plays*
	Indians
Jakov Lind	*The Silver Foxes Are Dead and other plays*
David Mercer	*On the Eve of Publication*
	After Haggerty
	Flint
John Mortimer	*The Judge*
	Five Plays
	Come As You Are
	A Voyage Round My Father
Joe Orton	*Crimes of Passion*
	Loot
	What the Butler Saw
	Funeral Games and *The Good and Faithful Servant*
	Entertaining Mr Sloane
Harold Pinter	*The Birthday Party*
	The Room and *The Dumb Waiter*
	The Caretaker

Harold Pinter	*A Slight Ache and other plays*
	The Collection and *The Lover*
	The Homecoming
	Tea Party and other plays
	Landscape and Silence
	Old Times
David Selbourne	*The Damned*
Jean-Paul Sartre	*Crime Passionnel*
Wole Soyinka	*Madmen and Specialists*
	The Jero Plays
Boris Vian	*The Empire Builders*
Peter Weiss	*Trotsky in Exile*
Theatre Workshop and Charles Chilton	*Oh What A Lovely War*
Charles Wood	*'H'*
	Veterans
Carl Zuckmayer	*The Captain of Köpenick*